SEAMARKS

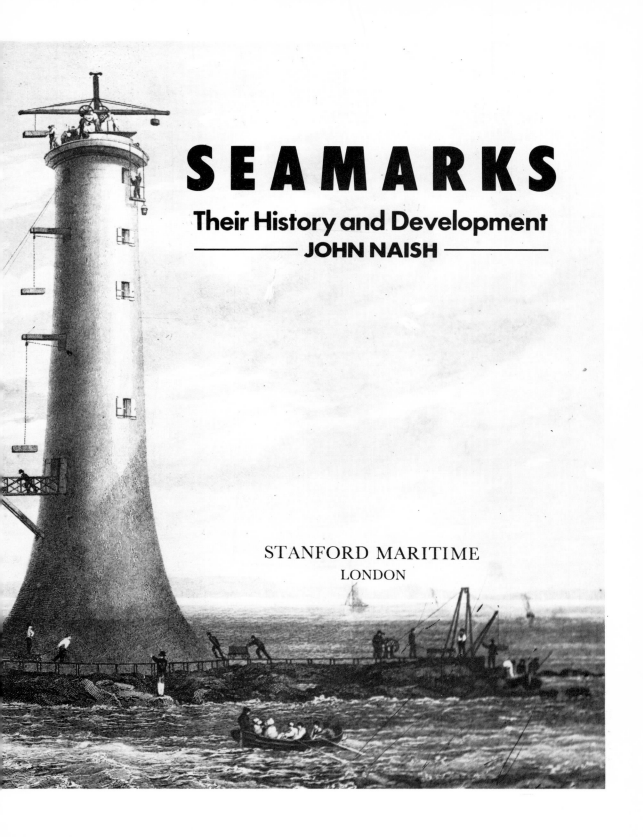

SEAMARKS

Their History and Development

JOHN NAISH

STANFORD MARITIME

LONDON

Stanford Maritime Limited
Member Company of the George Philip Group
12–14 Long Acre   London WC2E 9LP
Editor Phoebe Mason

First published in Great Britain 1985
Copyright © John M. Naish 1985

Set in Baskerville 11/12 by
Tameside Filmsetting Ltd., Ashton-under-Lyne, Lancashire
Printed in Great Britain by
Butler & Tanner Limited, Frome and London

British Library Cataloguing in Publication Data
Naish, John M.
    Seamarks: Their History and Development.
    1. Aids to Navigation
    I. Title
    627'.92   YK1013

ISBN 0-540-07309-1

Contents

Preface and Acknowledgements

A solitary night watch in a sailing boat is a good time to listen to the stars and to think. On a balmy June night in the North Sea, while two lightships and several buoys blinked out of the blackness signalling their characters, as it were their signatures, I thought 'when did this all begin?' I didn't think it was much more than a hundred years ago, but did Francis Drake have buoys to guide him as he weighed anchor in Plymouth Sound and slipped out into the Channel, or when he crept up to the Spanish Armada anchored off Gravelines? Perhaps he did, perhaps not. And what about all those wonderful beacons and transits I had just left behind in the Dutch seaways and the Frisian Islands, when did all that begin?

I began to visit libraries and turn to older and heavier encyclopaedias. It was no good: I required a reader's ticket at the National Maritime Museum in Greenwich to pursue my quest. At this point I would like to express my sincere thanks to the Curator and Library staff of the Museum for their help to me. Prof. Patrick McGrath, Emeritus Professor of History here in Bristol, put me in touch with one of his graduates, Dr Sean McGrail, to whom I would like to express my thanks for encouraging me to go on with the search. Dr McGrail and later Alan Stimson and Christopher Terrell in the Navigation Section of the Museum thought that no one had yet made a comprehensive study of the origin of seamarking, and this in itself, though frustrating my original intention to read all about it in a good book, persuaded me that perhaps it would be useful for others if I was to collect all the information together for possible publication. Being an amateur in the matter of historical research I needed a lot of help and I am most grateful to Alan Stimson and Christopher Terrell for suggesting lines of enquiry and methods of working.

At this point I received from an old friend in Hamburg, Heinz Schomann, A. W. Lang's beautifully illustrated book on the seamarking of the North Sea Coast of Germany and the Low Countries. Heinz Schomann, who taught my wife about English literature at grammar school and with whom I usually discuss questions of English poetry and history, provided me with more material on the early port history of Hamburg. Other German friends, Jörn and Elke Brumm of Hamburg and Ulrich Bauer of Copenhagen, have also helped me to obtain German and Danish books and papers, and I would like to thank them all. The late Ahrend Lang's book was both an inspiration and a model: I wish that he were still alive so that I could thank him, but I would like to acknowledge here the permission granted to me by Mrs Carola Lang to reproduce certain illustrations from the book.

I knew, of course, about Trinity House, having visited some lovely rock lighthouses in the course of youthful sailing adventures, but it was a great pleasure to step into the midst of history at Tower Hill, and to be given so much practical help and friendly encouragement from Paul Ridgway, the Public Relations Officer of Trinity House. He has guided me in my attempt to get up to date with all the developments in a modern Lighthouse Service and I am deeply grateful to him. Capt. Malcolm Edge, whom I met through my friend Michael Richards of Penzance, has been kindness itself. I would also like to thank Capt. Hookway of Trinity House Harwich, Jack Sharp of the Engineering Department there, Messrs B. Rodwell and E. D. Humphreys of the Research Section of the Engineer's Department at Tower Hill, and the officer in charge of the Dungeness Experimental Station who gave me so much of his time, wisdom and experience.

K. B. Fry, Secretary of the Port of Tyne Authority, kindly put me in touch with Grace McCombie of the Society of Antiquaries of Newcastle, who in her turn supplied me with material from Dodd's work on the Tyne leading lights, and I would like to thank both for their help. I would also like to thank Mr D. O. Le Conte of the States of Guernsey Ancient Monuments Committee for information on the origin of their local seamarks, Mr Henry Forssell of Helsinki for looking at the Finnish literature on my behalf, and Commander A. Holm of the Danish Marinens Bibliotek and E. Mørk Larsen of Søfartens Bibliotek for each giving me useful Danish references. Also W. F. J. Mörzer Bruyns of the Nederlands Scheepvart Museum and B. J. M. Grippeling of the Library of the Netherlands Ministry of Transport and Public Works, for helping me to find relevant material in the Dutch literature. Wolfgang Köberer of Frankfurt, the well-known expert on early astronomical navigation, generously helped me with advice. Dr Vibeka Evans of London was kind enough to translate some Danish passages into English, and Mr Wim Boere helped me with the Dutch works.

M. Jean Prunieras, Director of the Service des Phares et Balises, gave me some extremely useful advice on French sources and was kind enough to send me a copy of R. Faille's important work on eighteenth century French lights. I am also grateful to my old friend Dr Michel Bonduel of Paris, for obtaining useful material for me on recent French advances in automatic lighting and sea traffic control, as published by the Commission des Phares et Balises and the Department of Maritime Navigation.

The widow of the late H. Morcken who wrote about Europe's oldest

7

seamarks in Norway, Frau Guldborg Morcken, kindly sent me a reprint of her husband's paper with illustrations, for which I am most grateful. Her letter was motivated by a note requesting help which Brian Dolley allowed me to insert in *The Mariner's Mirror* and I thank him for this favour, which brought me several useful pieces of information and friendly help from such as Commander Richard Woodman, author of *Keepers of the Sea* and currently in command of the Trinity House Flagship *Patricia*. I would also like to thank Strahan Soames, editor of the *IALA Bulletin* for help and advice, and Norman Matthews of IALA Headquarters in Paris for reading that chapter of my manuscript which deals with the international search for uniformity in buoyage. No one could be more knowledgeable on the subject.

In travelling to the old seaports of England in the search for early material on beaconage, I was greatly helped by various archivists and librarians, notably Mrs P. Gill of the West Sussex Records Office and Mrs S. D. Thomson of Southampton. Mr R. E. Coley, Chief Executive of the Borough of Boston, put me in touch with the late John Bailey of the History of Boston Project which is housed in the Borough offices. Mr Bailey gave me a wonderful insight into the way a medieval port was managed and I was able to read in his offices extracts from an Elizabethan Charter which was concerned with improvements to beaconage.

In Kings Lynn, Dr Geoffrey Bolt, a keen local historian, helped me to contact the Harbour Master, museum authorities and librarian to all of whom I am most grateful for their time and friendly help. I am equally grateful to Mr and Mrs Ross Thompson of Boston for guiding my steps and for looking after me on my visit. I would also like to thank Mr John Collard, author of *The Maritime History of Rye* for sending me advice and suggestions based on his great knowledge of that ancient sea port.

Fellow enthusiasts and pharologists such as D. B. Hague and Christopher Nicholson have been generosity itself in giving me their time and friendly help. I would like to thank Douglas Hague for permission to reproduce two of the excellent maps, one of his photographs and three of his fine drawings, which have already appeared in *Lighthouses* by Hague and Christie. Christopher Nicholson, whose experience of watching the helicopter relief of rock lighthouses and lightships is quite unique, has kindly allowed me to reproduce some of his photographs.

Neville Long and D. W. Munro have also been most kind in helping me to trace or allowing me to reproduce certain illustrations from their respective books. The Northern Lighthouse Board and AB Pharos Marine Ltd (formerly AGA Navigation Aids Ltd) have both kindly provided me with illustrations of modern automated lighting installations. I am grateful also to Alan Peacock who has provided me with line drawings.

Rear Admiral Sir Edmund Irving, at one time Hydrographer of the Navy, gave much help and encouragement in the early stages of my work, and I would like to thank him most sincerely. My sister-in-law and her husband, Helmi and Fred Braches, helped me with translations from the Dutch and German. I would like to thank them both and also my old fellow student, collaborator in the writing of student reviews, and shipmate, Selwyn Taylor, who gave me the great benefit of his editorial and publishing experience by reading the whole manuscript with a critical eye. The creative ideas and suggestions he contributed have been adopted with gratitude, but I take full responsibility for all errors and omissions in the text.

I would finally like to thank Elizabeth Morgan, Dorothy Christmas and Marilyn Wright for much typing and deciphering of my scrawl. A great deal of this burden has also been carried by my wife, Barbara, who between her duties as a general practitioner, housewife and mother, has found time, often around midnight, to translate my handwritten sheets into legible type. Not only this, but she has translated works and written letters in German, and has tolerated and even sustained my enthusiam which must often have appeared totally ridiculous. She knows of my deep gratitude which I here record.

JOHN NAISH

Algars Manor
Iron Acton
Bristol

Foreword

Captain Sir Miles Wingate, KCVO, Deputy Master of Trinity House

The Author is to be congratulated on the amount of painstaking research that has obviously gone into the production of this book.

Tracing the history of aids to navigation from the time when man first 'went down to the sea in ships' must have been a mammoth task.

John Naish has written an authoritative book which will be of interest not only to those who venture upon the sea, but also to those who are fascinated by what can be a most hostile environment.

To be asked to write a Foreword for this fine work in the year 1985 gives me particular pleasure in view of the fact that this year these British Isles host the quinquennial Conference of the International Association of Lighthouse Authorities, a body which devotes itself to the ideal of making the seas of the world as safe as possible for all mariners.

I
Landmarks and Seamarks

Since man first took to the sea in boats, he was always seeking for landmarks to recognize. In some parts he could call to his aid bold headlands, white cliffs, or rocky stacks shaped on the anvil of the Earth's crust by the hammer blows of wind and water, to a shape which was instantly identifiable, even from far out to sea. At river mouths, he would look for the long sand or shingle spits of an estuary and the settlements within their shelter. Later, he would expect important river mouths to be marked by churches or temples, built on some prominent headland by sailors or merchants of an earlier generation who knew only too well the value of landmarks for the returning mariner.

Voyages three thousand years ago would have been mainly coastwise and the problem of 'finding the way' would have been in some respects easier than on land. Certainly in Northern Europe, which was mainly clothed in dense forest, the sea, the estuaries and the rivers were often the safest and quickest routes for travellers. Ancient land trackways tended to follow geological 'spines', either running for long distances along the upper contours of a range of hills, avoiding the dense bottom land of the valleys, or crossing swiftly over a watershed from one navigable river to another. To aid the land travellers of early cultures, 'sighting stones' or barrows were built on commanding ridges and straight transit lines were marked out by the surveyors or dod men, who used twin staves to line up their transit or 'ley' lines. Towers, forts and churches were later built along these ley lines, and at their intersections where settlements or markets were often situated. Thus a land traveller would be familiar with that same technique of local recognition which the sailor had long had to master. A church tower, visible for many miles above the trees, would indicate direction and give him assurance that he was nearing his destination.

The population of North Europe began to increase after the adoption of the mould board plough, which inverted the turf cleanly, making a good seedbed for the corn. Virgin lands came under the plough, new villages and settlements sprang up and tall buildings such as churches and windmills increased in number. The mariner came to rely on such man-made features: a hilltop wood framing a church spire,

a castle or a windmill placed high to catch the full force of the wind, would not only be used as marks of recognition but also perhaps as back markers for some foreground object like a rock or islet which, when seen in line with the distant mill or steeple, would either indicate hidden danger or show the line of a safe deep-water channel.

In such ways the seaman's knowledge of coastal topography was on a par with that of the landsman who usually had to traverse a country without roads or signposts. The seaman, however, had also to know about submerged rocks and sandbanks if he was not to risk his vessel. In this he was aided, before the age of charts or written sailing directions, by his accumulated knowledge of a coastline, which was related to the natural and man-made features he had learnt to recognize. Added to this was his seaman's eye, which could pick out the tidal swirl over a submerged reef or sense by the colour of the water the depth below. The sounding lead was also constantly in use. This simple instrument, consisting of a conical lead weight to the apex of which is attached a cord knotted at intervals of the length of a man's arm-span (six feet or a fathom) has hardly changed over the years. The leadsman, standing in the bows, casts the lead forward and lets the cord run out through his fingers until he feels the lead touch bottom. He then hauls it in while measuring the length of wetted cord, calls the depth back to the helmsman and makes another cast of the lead. Despite his reliance on the lead in coastal waters, how often must the early mariner have longed for some other mark in the sea or on its margin which would give warning of a shoal or help to fix his position when the light was dim or when fog rolled in to obscure the more distant landmarks.

The preamble to the Act VIII of Queen Elizabeth in 1566 shows clearly how the sailor, even of that comparatively developed era, relied upon his landmarks for coastal recognition: 'For as much as by the

A natural seamark. A rock pinnacle with white-painted top used as the front marker of a leading line at the entrance to St Mary's Harbour, Isles of Scilly.

The sixteenth century church of Notre-Dame at Roscoff is used as the back marker of a transit line for the harbour entrance.

taking away of certain steeples, woods and other marks standing upon the main shores adjoining to the sea coasts of the Realm of England and Wales, being as beacons and marks of ancient time accustomed for seafaring men, to save and keep them and the ships in their charge from sundry dangers thereto incident, divers ships with their goods and merchandises, in sailing from foreign parts to this Realm of England and Wales, and specially to the port and river of Thames, have by the lack of such marks of late years been miscarried, perished and lost in the sea, to the great detriment and hurt of the common wealth and the perishing of no small number of people.' So important were such landmarks to the coastal sailor that, in subsequent centuries, maritime communities often requested the repair of a ruined church steeple or tower and sometimes provided funds for the work. Even as late as 1737 the Trinity House of Kingston upon Hull, in England, paid £10 for repairing Kilnsea church steeple. Other churches and windmills on the shores of the Humber were vitally important to the pilots working ships in and out of this difficult river.

One of the great pioneers of coastal geography, Lewis Janzoon Waghenaer of the Netherlands, produced his charts and sailing directions for many important North European havens in the mid-sixteenth century, and his English translator A. Ashley, writing in 1583, made the following exhortation to Apprentices of the Art of Navigation: 'When so ever any Shipmaster or Mariner shall set forth from land out of any river or haven, diligently to mark what buildings, castles, towers, churches, hills, downes, windmills and other marks are standing upon the land, . . . all of which, or many of them, let him portray with his pen, how they bear and how far distant . . . '. Three hundred and ninety-one years later, the International Association of Lighthouse Authorities, after more than a hundred years of patient but frustrating effort by many such bodies, succeeded in obtaining world-wide acceptance of a uniform system of seamarks to warn of outlying dangers and to delineate safe-water channels in the approaches to coasts and harbours.

As a purely visual aid, a seamark is defined in the International Dictionary of Aids to Marine Navigation as 'an artificial or natural object of easily recognizable shape or colour or both, situated in such a position that it may be identified on a chart or related to a known navigational instruction.' This definition could have been acceptable to our seafaring ancestors except that charts did not become generally available until four hundred years ago. It now seems an appropriate time to recall the history of man's struggle to mark the dangers and the safeties of the sea, and to signpost the way between the most perilous part of a voyage to its tranquil end in a safe haven.

Sources for Chapter I

E. P. Edwards
C. G. Harris
A. Storey
E. G. R. Tayler
A. Watkins

II

Seamarks in the Ancient World

The Egyptians, the Phoenicians and the Romans were all traders by sea and it is not surprising that they sought to ease the problem of coastal recognition by building temples and fortresses in such a way as to help the homecoming sailor. Before the third century BC there may well have been pointed rocks, clifftop fires and island fortresses with easily recognizable features, but no records survive. From the third century BC we begin to get hints from early sources, some of them pictorial and artistic and some in recorded tradition, that the idea of a prominent tower illuminated by fire was already well known to those who lived near the sea and from the profits of the sea.

Then, between 283 and 277 BC, Sostratus of Cnidus built a structure that was so huge and so impressive in design that not only did it last for 1500 years, until finally destroyed by earthquakes, but it entered the mind and memory of the ancient and medieval world. This stepped tower was situated on the island of Pharos which then protected the harbour of Alexandria from the north. The colonaded base platform was 110 m square and raised 7 m above water level. The first section of the tower was 30 m square and built 72 m high, and contained a vast spiral ramp and many rooms; it was said to have been adorned with a cornice and statues of Tritons at the top. The second section was of octagonal section 17 m across and 35 m high through which the spiral continued. Above that there was a third, slightly shorter, cylindrical tower some 9 m across and 26 m high, which supported the 'lantern' housing the light and, according to legend, a 'reflector' and various scientific instruments. The Pharos tower to the statue of Poseidon at its top was over 140 m (about 500 ft) high; the only man-made structure higher at that time was the Great Pyramid of Cheops. Its height alone would justify inclusion as one of the seven wonders of the world, for it was not until steel-framed construction became possible at the end of the nineteenth century that any building rose higher. Apart from its height and its massive base, the Pharos tower must have been a wondrous building. Recent underwater exploration of its ruins has confirmed that it was probably decorated with sphinxes and several large statues, some of them 7 m tall. When we also consider that the internal ramps and stairs must have been built in such a way that animals or human slave gangs could haul up the masonry blocks for the upper parts, and that there must have been blocks and tackle, windlasses and other machinery for raising the topmost stones, we can see what a superb feat of architecture it was.

What was its purpose? The first and probably the most important reason for the vast expense of this undertaking was defence. The stepped nature of the tower and its commodious lower storey clearly made it the quarters of a considerable garrison, who could exercise and manoeuvre their projectiles either on the base platform or on the top of the first square tower. The second reason, subtly linked with defence, was prestige: the wealth and human resources of Ptolemaic Egypt were displayed in the Pharos for all to see. Such wealth and power was, to use our modern conception, a severe deterrent, not only to the opportunistic pirate but to the ambitions of other growing powers in the Mediterranean. The wonder of the Pharos soon became part of the folklore of expanding civilization, the Greek word became part of other European languages, and in its time it must have served its psychological purpose in bolstering and defending the power of Egypt. It was the pivot of a coastal signalling system, and the key to the defence of Alexandria; Caesar occupied it before attacking the city. The third, and for this study its most salient, purpose was to aid navigation.

A glance at the map of northern Egypt is sufficient to indicate to any mariner that coastal recognition must have been extremely difficult, if not impossible, in the approaches to the Delta of the Nile. Here the land

The Pharos at Alexandria, erected around 279BC and still in operation as a lighthouse when the Arabs took the city in the eighth century. Earthquakes and misguided demolition finally caused its destruction. The monumental building, reportedly of limestone, marble and red-brown Aswan granite, became known throughout the ancient and medieval world; this later representation is one of many which appeared on charts, documents and in art.

The Pharos of Alexandria during its long existence, based on research by E. M. Forster into all available sources including Arabic ones. Left: as it was thought to have been built. Of the ornamentation only the statue of Poseidon is shown. After the Moors took the city in the eighth century, an earthquake toppled the lantern. Demolition in search of a mythical treasure of Alexander reduced the tower to a relative stump with a fire on top. The Arabs made some restorations, and additions to the octagonal section (centre). In the 1100s another quake left only the lower storeys (right). The final earthquake in the 1300s destroyed the structure completely; a fort was later built on its foundations.

is all low-lying and anything likely to be visible from the deck of a galley 20 miles offshore would have been man-made. Tradition has it that from very ancient times there was a tower to mark a main channel into the Nile. Knowing the proven value of such a tower to the offshore mariner, the authorities of Alexandria would have appreciated the importance of height: indeed, the geometrical and astronomical knowledge of the Egyptians would have qualified them to predict the exact distance from which the top of the Pharos tower would have been visible from the deck of a vessel. They would also have known that rare indeed are the atmospheric conditions which allow an object to be seen from 60 sea miles away, though mountains with snow on them or active volcanoes could be seen from even farther away. Etna and Vesuvius must have been valuable seamarks to the early Phoenician, Greek and Roman navigators, so the idea of lighting a fire on a hilltop, a cliff or an artificial tower would have been long known. In lower Egypt, where a long, low and featureless coastline faced the sailor returning from the mountainous shores of Sicily, Crete and the Aegean, such a high tower with a smoke plume might have been picked up in clear conditions from as far away as 60 miles, which was surely enough for an oar-propelled galley. At night, a glow reflected from clouds might be seen before any direct light from the fire itself. We have no idea what fuel was burnt at the top of the Pharos tower, but it seems probable, from the construction of the internal ramps and the flat surfaces, that large stores of wood or papyrus bundles were kept. Slaves, controlled by military personnel, would have served the fire.

Other fire towers followed throughout the Mediterranean. Important strategic points, such as those near Antioch in the Gulf of

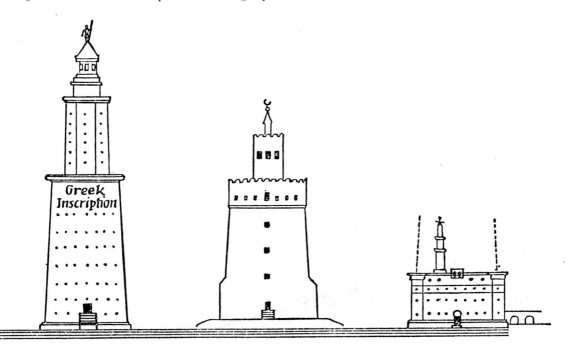

Greek
Inscription

Iskenderum and those commanding the Sea of Marmora and the Hellespont, were served by such towers before the beginning of the first century BC. Antioch was a Byzantine city on a river mouth and commanded the coastal route from the Byzantine Empire (now Turkey) to Syria, Mesopotamia and Egypt.

As the Romans began to be dominant in the Mediterranean and to apply their ruthless efficiency to the problems of sea trade, artificial harbours were built at Ostia near Rome and Leptis Magna in Libya. They incorporated a fortified fire tower, either built on the end of a protective mole or, as in the case of Ostia, on a sunken ship filled with stone and concrete in the mid-channel of the entrance. The designers of the Mulberry Harbours on the invasion beaches of Normandy were doing nothing new! A list of Roman fire towers with their locations is given in the table at the end of this Chapter. The evidence derives from written records such as those of Pliny, bas-reliefs, decorations on lamps and vases, mosaics and from coins.

The Roman Empire had encompassed not only North Africa and West Asia but also Spain, France and parts of Britain. Beyond the Mediterranean, there is sound evidence that the Romans either built on an earlier Phoenician tower at Gades (Cadiz) or built a new one, and that Cepio in the second century built a tower on a stony bank offshore at Chipionia, on the south point of the entrance to the Guadalquivir River leading to Sevilla. They do not seem to have thought it necessary to mark the entrance to the Tagus, good and secure harbour though it is, but at the northwest extremity of Spain they built a substantial tower commanding the entrance to La Coruña and Ferrol known as Julio Briga. This tower appears in early sailing instructions and primitive charts of the Middle Ages, but it is doubtful whether it was continually in service. However, enough of it remained for it to be restored as a defensive tower in the fourteenth century and as a light tower in the seventeenth century (see Chapter VII). This site off La Coruña has the distinction of being a known and cared-for seamark for close on 1500 years, and for long periods of its history it was lit.

To the north, and in furtherance of their military aim of subduing the troublesome Celtic tribes of Britain, Claudius and Caligula are credited with building two fire towers on either side of the Straits of Dover. The one above the present city of Boulogne and known for thousands of years as the Tour d'Ordre must have been defensive and military in purpose, for from the purely navigational point of view it was built unnecessarily high and on an elevated site. The same is true of the tower at Dover, now enclosed by the ramparts of Dover Castle. What was the point, one wonders, of building a four-storey masonry tower with wooden floors when the base of the tower already stood some 40m above sea level, ample elevation for visibility from the French coast? Did the Romans not know about the British climate and the low sea fogs of Dover, or did they build the tower primarily as a defensive bastion for a permanent garrison? It seems likely that, as with the Pharos tower of Alexandria, prestige, defence and navigation were the mixed reasons for the building of these towers.

The Roman Pharos at Dover standing within Dover Castle. (F. K. Zemke, Deutsche Leuchttürme)

The question of the upkeep of lights on Roman towers is answered, not by any surviving documents for there are none, but by the structure and function of the towers. They were military and political instruments in a totalitarian state, staffed by soldiers who commanded a body of locally recruited slaves. Fire-keeping was not the problem for the Romans that it was later to be for the medieval authorities.

We know very little about Roman buoyage and beaconage, though we know that they built wooden signal towers which could also have been used either as single seamarks or as part of a leading line. There is no record of towers used as beacons, and of a temple dedicated to Diana of Ephesus being used as a seamark for entry to the Rhone delta. It is clearly in such estuarine waters that the use of beacon poles and tree branches would have started. We know that the inhabitants of early Venice, who were refugees from the civil and military chaos of the

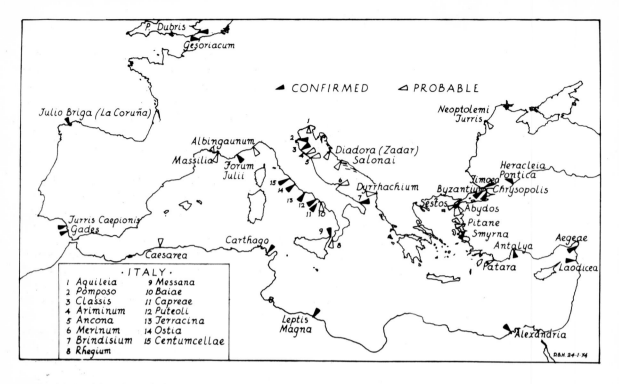

◄ CONFIRMED   ◅ PROBABLE

· ITALY ·

1 Aquileia	9 Messana
2 Pomposo	10 Baiae
3 Classis	11 Capreae
4 Ariminum	12 Puteoli
5 Ancona	13 Terracina
6 Merinum	14 Ostia
7 Brindisium	15 Centumcellae
8 Rhegium	

Lighthouses of the classical world. (Hague and Christie, Lighthouses)

mainland which had followed the collapse of Rome and the invasions from the North, had become expert at erecting buildings on detached mudbanks by driving vertical piles into the mud and achieving a firm base for wood, stone or brick structures. It is inconceivable that they would not also have used vertical pole beacons to mark the edges of the fairly narrow channels which criss-crossed the lagoon. There was a plentiful supply of timber to be cut in the war-ravaged mainland north of the lagoon, and from time to time the Venetians exercised territorial authority over these forest areas. The delta of the River Po was also suitable for channel marking by pole beacons, but there is no positive evidence that channel-marking buoys were used. However, in a thirteenth century book of sailing directions (known in Italy as a *portolano*) which was called *La Compasso da Navigare*, there is a reference to buoys in the Guadalquivir River, which runs a tortuous course through the Marismas from Sevilla to the Atlantic near Chipionia. Directions were that, when entering the river, the sailor should take soundings and then follow the buoys upstream when the tide served.

These early portolans of medieval times not only give some indications of the beacon towers which were built to facilitate entry to the rival ports of Genoa and Pisa but include the first reference to the use of leading marks. Thus, in the approach to Pisa, then at the mouth of the Arno, the end of the harbour wall held in view between two towers in the town gave a safe approach between rocks on either hand. In the Levant, the safe approach to the port of Acre was on a bearing which held the Constable's house in line with the Tower of the Flies.

(Acre was the scene of a famous siege in Crusader times, and is now in Israel.)

As the post-Roman period of chaos began to end, with the rise of Charlemagne and the later infusion of vigorous seafaring blood from Scandinavia, there is evidence of sporadic endeavours to aid navigators and to defend strategic waterways. Tradition has it that the beacon tower on the island of Corduan in the mouth of the Garonne River was built by Louis the Pious, son of Charlemagne, in the ninth century. Certainly this tower, which had provision for a fire on top, served the dual purpose of coastal defence and navigational aid in a river which was so important for the wine trade. In the Mediterranean, a tower was built on the offshore shoal of Meloria in 1157 by the Pisans, but it was later destroyed during the maritime rivalry between Genoa and Pisa. The Genoese had built their own fire tower in the twelfth century, the Lanterna of Genoa, which was later greatly enlarged and became famous in the medieval world. After Porto Pisano silted up, Genoa became the dominant maritime influence in the western Mediterranean. The light tower near Messina was re-established in the Crusader times, while the Venetians built several navigational towers on the Lido in the same period. Louis IX of France built a military tower with a light at Aigues Mortes, which was his point of departure for one of the later Crusades in 1246. This Tour de Constance still stands, but is now some miles inland.

In the Dark Ages of North Europe monastic groups and hermits had taken to remote islands and premontories where their work of succour for shipwrecked sailors became mixed with the salvage of wreck goods and the showing of candle lights in chapel windows. During the Viking raids of the tenth century even these poor and isolated communities often fell prey to the raiders, but their work somehow went on: there is good medieval evidence of lights being displayed in several strategically placed chapels or hermit houses in Southern Ireland, notably Hook Head off Waterford, in Cornwall, around Rye and Winchelsea, at Great Yarmouth, on Spurn Head at the mouth of the Humber and on Hunstanton Cliffs in the approaches to The Wash and Lynn Harbour.

The Vikings themselves are not revealed by structural remains to have been great builders of navigational aids, but sea traffic may have been sparse and very local. Most of those which are known to have been built were on Norway's southern coast. Floke Vilgeursson, the discover of Iceland, had a stone tower built at Smørsund, which was referred to in the Sagas of Flokavardi but is now known as Smørsund Varde. Close to this a stone cross was placed on the island of Kvitsøy, which was used as a seamark. Further south, at Ny Hellesund on the southern extremity of Norway, there were in historical times twin stone towers said to have been built by King Olav Haraldsson (St Olaf) in the early eleventh century. In the same period, a stone cross used as a seamark was built at Korssund in the approaches to the Sognefjord: it marked the entrance to a narrow, well sheltered harbour of refuge used perhaps as a rendevous for raiding parties or trading fleets leaving for or

The stump of one of the twin towers of Ny Hellesund built by King Olaf, 1015–30. (R. Morcken)

returning from the North Sea. Tønsberg in the vicinity of Oslo takes its name from a seamark surmounted by a *tonne* or barrel. This was a wooden structure later incorporated in a stone tower.

Farther east, in the Baltic, the greater ease of transport by water than by land, and the topography and lack of tide, were such as to encourage the Scandinavian and Wendish to use birch branches and larger poles to mark the channels between islands and within river mouths. However, there are neither historical records nor illustrations to throw

The Korssund Cross seamark erected in the eleventh century. (R. Morcken)

light on the matter. The building of fire towers and leading marks came after the Drang nach Ostern when the Teutonic peoples took over from the Wendish in the region now known as Poland, Lithuania and Latvia. Developments in ship design had allowed sailing vessels to come into their own as carriers and East-West trade was beginning to grow.

Roman Fire Towers in the Early Empire Period

Roman port	Present name	Location
Ostia	Ostia (now inland	Mouth of Tiber, W Italy
Puteoli	Pozzuoli	Bay of Naples, W Italy
Capreae	Capri	Bay of Naples, W Italy
Terracina	Artficial harbour	W Italy
Centumcellae	Artificial harbour	W Italy
Cape Pelorus	Messina district	NE Sicily
Forum Julii	Fréjus	Côte d'Azur, S France
Carthago	Carthage	Tunisia
Leptis Magna	Artificial harbour	Homs, Libya
Aegeae	Antioch district	Turkey
Lao Dicea	Latakia	Syria
Brindisium	Brindisi	heel of Italy
Pomposo	near Ravenna (now inland)	Adriatic coast, Italy
Classis	near Ravenna (now inland)	Adriatic coast, Italy

Smyrna	Izmir	Turkey
Byzantium	Istanbul	Turkey
Chrysopolis	Istanbul	Turkey
Heracleia Pontica		Black Sea coast of Turkey
Gades	Cadiz	Atlantic coast of Spain
Turris Caepionis	Chipiona (mouth of Guadalquivir)	Atlantic coast of Spain
Julio Briga	La Coruña	Atlantic coast of Spain
Gesoriacum	Tour d'Ordre, Boulogne	France
P. Dubris	Dover	England

Sources for Chapter II

D. Adams
D. B. Hague and R. Christie
H. Morcken
J. J. Norwich
E. G. R. Taylor
D. W. Waters

III

The Hanseatic League and the Organization of Seamarks 1250–1550

Although the greatest expansion of sea trade ever known took place in the two centuries following the voyages of Vasco da Gama and Christopher Columbus, the steady growth of both nautical skills and mercantile organization in the Middle Ages had already laid down a platform for this 'great leap forward'.

The centres of medieval growth were in two widely separated areas of influence. Venice, arising out of the ruin and decay of the Roman Mediterranean 'common market', was able to establish a monopolistic stranglehold on oriental trade during and after the Crusades. Secondly, there was the Hanseatic League. Although the Venetians, and later the Genoans, were certainly the leaders in commercial practices based on strict observance of customary law, there is little evidence that in early medieval times they were great innovators in methods of ship construction, ship propulsion and navigation. The island-strewn, tideless Mediterranean set no severe problems of coastal recognition and dead reckoning, while its unpredictable winds made sailors cling to the oar-propelled galley for much longer than the Northern peoples clung to their Viking-style boats. The latter, faced with the swift tides and currents of the lower Rhine and the great Frisian estuaries of the German Bight, the rarely calm and often stormy waters of the open North Sea and the English Channel, experimented more freely with different methods of ship construction and began to build boats solely for sail propulsion and greater cargo-carrying and seakeeping capacity. They rapidly adopted the stern-mounted rudder when the technical problems of fitting this into the hull had been overcome. The medieval cog which evolved for trading was single-masted with rounded bow and stern. It was a versatile ship capable of sailing in deep or shallow water, which could take the ground safely if stranded or when unloading cargo, and which was sufficiently manoeuvrable under sail in tideways. It was round-bottomed and had the high-sided profile which made it a profitable cargo carrier.

More efficient ships allowed the Northern merchants to trade in bulk goods. The problems facing them were similar to those of the Venetians: how to organize the commerce, how to suppress or at least contain piracy, and how to minimize losses by storm and stranding. To surmount these problems the merchants and mariners of the Baltic and North Sea evolved the Hanseatic League, a commercial and legal confederation of city-states which subscribed to the same code of trade practices for their mutual benefit.

Although there may have been no formal link between the Venetian traders and those of that other great trading centre of the north, Novgorod, it is highly probable that familiarity with the trading practices of the Venetians would have been gained through the network of European sea and river traders, and that the first commercial codes of the early Hanseatic merchants derived from the example of Venice. Furthermore, it seems, from a comparison of the sea distances and tidal flows recorded in all the early books of sailing directions, that the Italian shippers of the Mediterranean must have met and been familiar with the North Sea traders. Their books of sailing directions, known in Italy as *portolanos*, in France as *routiers*, in Germany as *Seebücher* and in English as *sea rutters*, shared common descriptions and details of coastal features. It is probable that the most frequent points of contact were in Flanders, for both Antwerp and Sluys-Bruges were the greatest mercantile ports of Middle Europe in these times. There the ships and sailors from Venice and Genoa met the merchant adventurers of the Hanse.

The small towns of the Baltic had no political autocracy within whose shelter they could develop commercial practices; there was no common law, and they were subject to a great variety of feudal overlords. It is therefore remarkable that they were able, acting solely under the stimulus of their shared interest in free and lawful trade, to evolve a co-operative system which was a forerunner of future democratic practice. At first, the capital of this commercial world was Visby on the island of Gotland in the eastern Baltic: here mercantile records were kept and silver money was coined that was so trustworthy that it was named, after the common name for the Hanseatic traders, 'Osterling' silver, later just 'Sterling'. In the fourteenth century Lübeck, because best suited by its geographical position in the southwest Baltic to hold the balance between the raw material exporters of the East and the early manufacturers of the West, became the unofficial capital of the Hanseatic League. From the records of Lübeck we can see the gradual evolution of systems of payment, monetary exchange, tolls and taxes for use of harbours, banking, and insurance of cargoes. Driven by the sanction of commercial boycott, the cities of the Hanse had to agree on many subjects: among these we can find the first traces of a common interest in the provision of fixed navigational aids for sailors entering and leaving harbours and river mouths.

The problem, as seen by the merchant and ship-owner of the thirteenth century, was a mixture compounded of suppression of piracy, salvage of wreck goods and the provision of seamarks. Thus, the burghers of Hamburg agreed in 1300 on a considerable capital adventure in the dangerous north-facing mouth of the Elbe. Here the land is all low-lying, and the deep-water channel is flanked by many miles of sand, mudbanks and stony reefs. It was abominably difficult for a ship's captain to find the entrance to the river, let alone to keep within the deep-water channel, especially when the prevailing north-westerly wind was blowing into, and meeting, the massive outflow from one of the largest rivers in Europe. The Scharhoorn reef, just to seaward of a large sand island, was the commonest danger on which ships came to grief. It was therefore decided to build on this sand island a tower and small fort, to be constructed of a granite block base surmounted by a timber structure faced with bricks. This was intended to house and shelter (under what conditions of discomfort we can only guess at) an official of the Hanse-Stadt Hamburg and ten men, whose duties were to salvage wreck goods, rescue shipwrecked sailors, report sightings of pirate vessels and possibly to keep a signal fire on the summit of the tower when circumstances demanded. The decision had been taken after prolonged deliberations in the Rat Haus and after permission had been granted by the territorial ruler of the area, the Herzog von Sachsen-Lauenburg, one Landesherr von Hadeln. The building was not completed and occupied until 1310.

The early history of the island tower and refuge is patchy, but it was called in the current language of Plattdeutsch or Low German Dat Nige Wark, which means the New Works or New Building. Subsequently it was known by its High German equivalent, Neuwerk, and this is the name it carries to this day. Throughout the fourteenth and fifteenth century it appears that the approaches to the Elbe were plagued by pirates who seemed often to have their bases in the East Frisian Islands or in Denmark. In 1525 a notorious pirate and Danish 'Admiral', Klaus Kniphof, was captured and executed by a force raised in Hamburg, and thereafter the task of placing further navigational aids in the approaches and in the river itself was tackled with more vigour. The garrison of the Neuwerk tower had long been authorized to identify passing ships, so that tolls for passing the mouth of the Elbe could be levied in harbour, but there is no evidence of systematic seamarking before the mid-sixteenth century. A tonne buoy sited north

Lorich's 1568 drawing of the Neuwerk Tower and its Hamburg Bake with barrel topmark. (A. W. Lang, Geschichte des Seezeichenwesens*)*

of the Scharhoorn is recorded in 1466, but it may not have been regularly on station.

There were peculiar geographical features in the coastline of the North German plain, through which flowed not only the water of great rivers like the Schelde, the Meuse and the Rhine (which themselves linked together in a great tangle of delta channels), but also the rivers Elbe, Weser and Ems, which had to find their way into the North Sea through the chain of the Frisian sand-dune islands. This infinitely complex and changing system of waterways, marshland and estuary was crying out to be marked and signposted. Just when this began, and how, is not known. The probability is that early man used the conveniently shaped birch branches to show the edges of mud banks and shallows. They are still used throughout Northern Europe as easily visible, cheap and readily available waymarkers, not only in tidal waters or on the inner sides of the bends of inland rivers but also on the featureless snow plains and plateaux of Scandinavia. Certainly these branches, known in Dutch and German as *Pricken* and in English as withies, were used in addition to the larger and stronger pole beacons which were suitable for the more exposed positions.

The Hansestadt Bremen organized some system of buoyage and beaconage within the River Weser and its approaches at an early date, indeed there are records of buoys there as early as the eleventh century. The approaches to Rostock at Warnemünde were marked by a single buoy in the thirteenth century. Fire towers and candle lanterns had been established at the entrances to several Baltic harbours by 1500 (*vide infra*).

The approaches to Sluys and Brüge (Bruges) from the outer estuary of the Schelde were probably first buoyed in the eleventh or twelfth

Chart of entrance to the River Swin near Sluys. Drawn by an unknown artist about 1500, this is the earliest chart showing Seetonnen. *The fourteenth century battle of Sluys took place in the vicinity. The importance of Bruges and the shallowness of the Swin made buoyage a necessity. Note that the villages shown are now well inland. (A. W. Lang,* Geschichte des Seezeichenwesens)

century, for Bruges was the most important entrepot of the Hanseatic trade. The oldest surviving chart of the coastal entrance is from about 1500 and shows two buoyed channels, either side of a middle-ground sandbank called De Looppinghe, both of which channels lay west of the island of Kadzant. The villages and churches of Knocke and St Anna ter Muiden are shown and the chart is named 'Swin bei Sluis'. The Swin or Zwin was then the waterway to Bruges: Sluys and ter Muiden, which are now many miles inland, were then coastal.

Another early navigational aid in Flanders was a tall tower dating from the thirteenth or fourteenth centuries, on the top of which a fire of reed bundles could be lit and which stood within the entrance to the River Yser at Nieuwpoort. This was still standing as a ruin in the nineteenth century, for it appears in a lithograph of 1822.

Throughout Flanders, the Netherlands, Frisia and the great rivers of the German bight, in the period 1100–1300, townships began to develop institutions capable not only of organizing the manufacture and positioning of buoys and beacons, but of collecting tolls from the ships which used their channels and harbours. A buoy was constructed on the barrel principle with staves bound by iron hoops and it was therefore known by the same name: *Tonne* means barrel in both German and Dutch. Beacons were known as *Baken*, and the more sophisticated timber structures erected on islands or dunes to act as leading marks were known as *Kapen*, or sometimes in Dutch or Plattdeutsch, *Caapen*. The tolls which the ship's captain had to pay were known as Tonnen, Baken and Kapen Geldes, or more simply Tonnengeld, and were levied in harbour on a scale dependent on the value of the cargo rather than the size of the ship. The use of the word 'tonnage' for the cargo capacity of a ship derives from the number of standard barrels she could carry. The administration of this taxation must have been extremely elaborate, and it is illuminating to ponder on the sophistication of some of these medieval fiscal arrangements, especially when one considers that they used only quill pens, parchment, ink and sealing wax for recording and copying.

As far as the organization involved in the construction, positioning fixing and laying of Tonnen and Baken, boatyards were established for the manufacture, repair and storage of equipment. The boats used for driving-in Baken and laying Tonnen were first known as Bargia, later Bardze and finally Bardse. The officer responsible was a semi-military official known as a Barsenmeister and under him served a Tonnenleger (buoy-layer) and Bakenstecker (beacon-fixer). Because of the risk of pirates the boats had some armament, and gradually they evolved to a more specialized construction as the exposed outer channels came to be marked. The crew acted as river police as well as mark-fixers. Presumably they also tried to prevent the stealing of wreck goods from stranded ships, and the Barsenmeister's evidence would be called for in the frequent legal disputes arising from the disappearance of cargoes from such ships.

Early charts of the sixteenth century show fixed marks of Baken and Kapen type in the approaches to many Baltic cities such as Danzig,

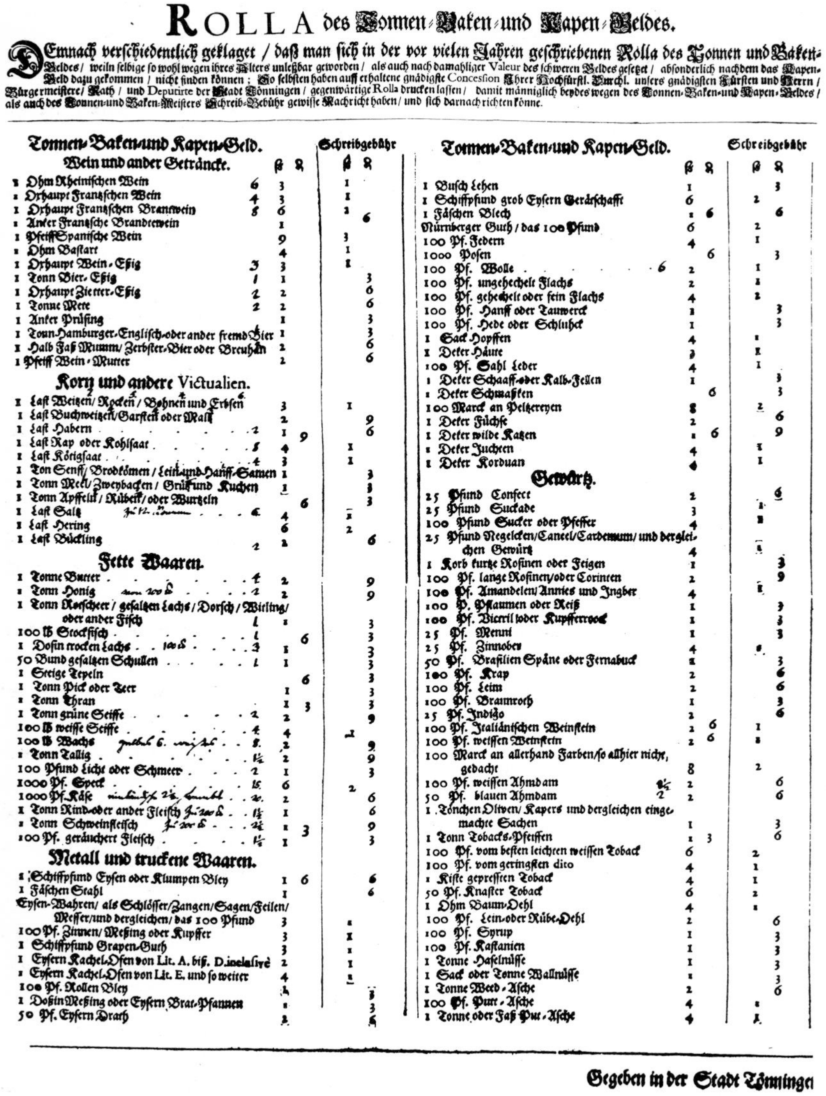

ROLLA des Tonnen-Baken-und Kapen-Geldes.

(Fraktur tariff document, dated 1682, listing cargo items and their Tonnen-, Baken- und Kapen-Geld dues in columns. Text largely illegible.)

Part of the cargo tariff for levying 'Tonnen, Baken und Kapen Geldes', dated 1682. This shows that seamarking dues were levied on the value of the cargo shipped. (A. W. Lang, Geschichte des Seezeichenwesens)

Gegeben in der Stadt Tönningen

Rostock and Stralsund. Archaeological evidence suggests that there was a hilltop beacon fire at Kolabacken (Coal Hill) near Falsterbo point in 1220.

In 1429 the Danish King imposed a levy, the Sound Dues, on all vessels passing through the narrow Sound of Helsingør (Elsinore) which was the safest route between the North Sea and the Baltic and lay between Sjaelland and Sweden. This route was fast becoming one of the most important navigation channels in the world, but at first it appears that the Danes extracted money without providing a service. Then, about 1520, the Danish Crown began to organize the laying of buoys in the fairway opposite Copenhagen. Forty years later King Frederick II ordered the marking of the whole passage from Skagen at

A sea chart of 1642 of the approaches to the River Ems; pole beacons, buoys and twin kapen on the island of Bant are shown and also the substantial masonry tower on Borkum. An earlier chart is shown in Chapter VI. (A. W. Lang, Geschichte des Seezeichenwesens*)*

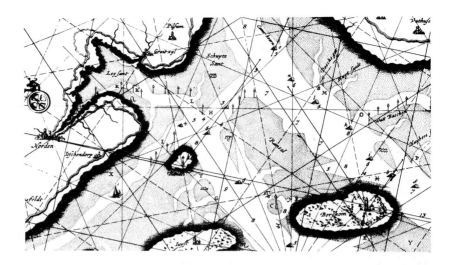

the northern tip of Denmark through the Sound of Helsingør to Falsterbo. Lights were placed on Skagen, Anholt and Kullen (*vide infra*) while buoys were laid off the reefs of Skagen, Anholt, Salthom and Falsterbo. The Sound Dues provided a steady source of income for this work.

The combination of birch branch besoms as topmarks on pole beacons, which is so characteristic of Danish waters today, may have originated locally or further to the east in the Baltic. A bundle of birch twigs was bound together by their stems, as in the making of a rustic besom (broom), and placed atop the straight pole marking the edge of the channel. At some stage the poles marking the north side of a channel were differentiated from those on the south side by having the point of the besom down, those on the opposite side having the point up. Other recognition topmarks included wicker baskets, small barrels or wooden crowns. The idea spread to the North Sea and the West, though for many years the Bakensteckers of Germany seemed to prefer round topmarks known as *Kugeltopfzeichen*. For outlying pole beacons or those marking a separation of channels, a small barrel or wicker cage was often used so that the incoming mariner could recognize the silhouette from a distance.

The marking of the coasts and inland seaways of the Netherlands began early in the Middle Ages and there is every reason to believe that the local sailors and fishermen were pioneers in different methods of channel marking by pole beacons and tonnen. There is also a long local tradition of building small huts equipped with fire platforms on prominent dunes so as to give navigational assistance to the fishing fleet. These *Vuurboeten* were a feature of the North Sea coast. The town of Brielle at the mouth of the River Maas seems to have been a leader in this for there are records from 1280 of two fire towers so aligned as to give safe passage by night into the harbour, and also, from the same date, there is a record of ships having to pay a toll known as Caap en Vierboetrecht for the upkeep of these relatively sophisticated marks.

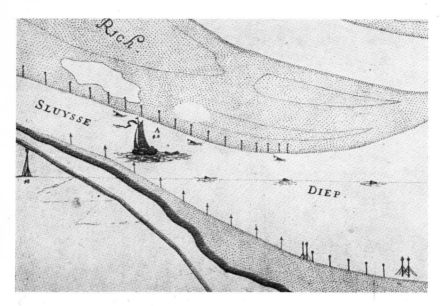

Pole beacons and a land beacon at the mouth of the Sluysse Diep at the mouth of the River Maas. Note 'lateral' topmarks. (A. W. Lang, Geschichte des Seezeichenwesens)

Reliable records from the sixteenth century indicate that these twin seamarks were frequently out of commission, however, due to accidental fires, dismantling in times of war, lack of reliable keepers and lack of money to repair or rebuild them.

Despite the pioneering spirit of the Dutch sailors and fishermen, there is evidence from the fifteenth century that the sturdy independence of the ports and towns led to difficulties in harmonizing the system of seamarking. Thus, we find in 1495 the Emperor Maximilian issuing an ordinance to force the authorities of Dordrecht, Brielle and Rotterdam to meet and agree on matters of common interest, such as the methods of salting fish and the marking of channels. It is not until 1578 that a college of pilotage was set up which included in its remit the regulation and financing of beaconage and buoyage.

Hanseatic merchants had an important depot and counting house at the Steeleyard in London, which dealt with wool exports and English imports of hemp, timber and tar. There was also a thriving English wool and textile trade with Flanders, but there is no historical evidence that the medieval merchants of London concerned themselves with the marking of channels into the Port of London.

This was not the case with the ports of Lynn and Boston, on the Wash, in both of which the Hanse had established steeleyardes. Here there is evidence that the Osterlings, as the Baltic traders of the Hanse were still known, had imported some of their expertise in seamarking into these English East Coast ports. In the thirteenth century Boston was such a busy port that it collected a third of all the Custom duties payable to the Crown. Having, like the North German and Flemish harbours, a difficult approach through shifting sandbanks, it is probable that the same methods of channel marking with birch branches or taller beacon poles were used. Certainly the Charter of Queen Elizabeth granted to the burghers of Boston in the fourteenth year of her reign (1572) refers to the beacons and marks, 'all which things are nowe almost utterly decayed'. The Charter of 1572 was a remarkable example of devolution of government, for it had become apparent to Elizabeth that, as long as all the Rights of Admiralty were in the hands of some Court favourite, Boston lacked the means to keep the seaways marked. The Charter, therefore, gave to Boston the Rights of Admiralty, the power to impose fines and levy tolls on shipping which entered the port or anchored in the Boston or, as it was then known, the Norman Deeps. In its preamble, the Charter states that all ships 'have great refuge and succour . . . in certain places commonly called the Norman Deepes'. Shipwreck and disasters 'for the most part arise by the lack of sufficient number of seamarks in the said place called the Norman Deepes'. The burghers of Boston were commanded 'to assure and take upon them from time to time for every hereafter to build uppe, repairs and susteyne at their own proper costs and charge' the marking of the Knock and Dogs Head Sand, Wanfleet Haven and Pully Head. In 1577 the port charges were 1s 8d for English ships, 4s for Scots, 5s for 'strangers' and 3s 4d for wool carriers. Colliers paid about a shilling. The burghers paid one of their number to erect and maintain the beacons.

By the time of the accession of the Tudors the English had lagged far behind the Dutch, not only in ship design and building but also in techniques of sea marking. Early Hampshire, Sussex and Cinque Port records tell a story of continual bickering and litigation over acts of piracy and theft of wreck goods. The culprits were often foreigners from France or the Spanish Netherlands, the notorious Dunkirkers foremost among them, but quite frequently the pirates and wreck-thieves were other Englishmen. The medieval rivalry between the fishermen of Yarmouth and the Cinque Ports led to fighting, the illegal arrest of ships and lawsuits. The problems of piracy and wreck-salvage seem to have occupied so much of the attention of the South Coast mariners that no thought was given to seamarking. Certainly, there is no mention in their local records either of the fixing or repairing of beacons and buoys.

The Tudors, who were aware of the chaotic state of maritime organization, tried to control matters by a system of regional Vice Admirals responsible to the Lord High Admiral (a political appointment) for their own section of coast. Records suggest that most of the Admiralty Court's time was taken up with litigation resulting from the prevailing lawlessness at sea, but these courts did at least provide an administrative basis for the control of piracy and punishment of sea-thieves and wreckers, and perhaps also for the improvement of havens and the marking of dangers. The basis was there, but we do not know whether much was done. Admiralty Courts were a source of revenue from the fines and tolls which could be legally demanded. Some of the profit found its way back to the Lord High Admiral, most stayed in the hands of the Vice Admiral and some may have been spent on improvements. Many of the larger self-governing ports petitioned to be granted Rights of Admiralty and in the case of

Boston, as we have seen, the price of devolution was an obligation to maintain and develop 'signs of the sea'.

It seems very probable, but by no means certain, that port authorities such as Southampton's, to whom Rights of Admiralty were eventually granted, did nothing about seamarks. Southampton had suffered economically from Henry VIII's attempt to stop the export of raw wool from Britain's outports, to channel all raw wool through the Calais Staple and to build up the finished cloth trade, most of which had to pass through the port of London. Genoan and Venetian shipmasters who had been used to carry wool from Southampton no longer bothered to bring their cargoes of wine, silk and oil, since there was no certainty of a return cargo. Thus the attempt to rationalize maritime trade, suppress piracy and enforce the payment of customary dues through regional Vice Admirals was in many ways unsuccessful.

It is against this background that the granting of Henry VIII's first Charter to Trinity House of Deptford Strond must be seen. The merchants and mariners of London seem to have resisted pressure from foreign shipmasters to seamark the Thames Estuary. There was always the fear of sharing the secrets of the channels which led to strategic harbours such as London, Chatham and Harwich. Thames pilots used prominent hills, cliffs, woods, windmills and church towers such as that of Reculver as transit lines to fix their position relative to the sandbanks. These, together with continuous sounding, were no doubt satisfactory in perfect weather, but when fog obscured the coast or there was an onshore wind blowing, the mariner must have longed for some other navigational aids.

The Charter of 1514 established Trinity House as a royally approved pilotage authority and professional body in which one of the King's most trusted maritime experts, Sir Thomas Spert, played a leading role. Henry's son, Edward VI, completed the secularization by incorporating Trinity House, and in 1566 Elizabeth gave them the lucrative Rights of Ballastage under which all shipmasters taking on ballast from the Thames Estuary had to pay appropriate dues to the Corporation. Without this revenue the Brethren of Trinity House would not have been able to bear the expense of improving seamarking, which was specifically enjoined upon them by the Act of 1566. There was some doubt as to whether this entitled them to put seamarks in the water, though they were clearly made responsible for marks upon the land. In Elizabeth's final Charter, granted to Trinity House in 1593, their obligation and duty to mark the channels was specifically inscribed and their primacy in matters of seamarking was established.

By the end of Queen Elizabeth's reign, which coincided approximately with the beginning of the seventeenth century, a strong wind of change was blowing through England's maritime affairs. Not only were the shipbuilders of Chatham, London and countless smaller ports catching up with the Dutch, but educated, intelligent and influential men were giving their whole minds to the seafaring arts. The Corporation of Trinity House, rising from its obscure ecclesiastical and

Reculver Church, 'the steeples whereof shooting up their lofty spires stand the mariner in good stead as markers whereby they avoid certain sands and shelves in the mouth of the Tamis' (W. Camden, 1610). Built on the old Roman fort of Reculbium, Reculver has been a seamark from ancient times.

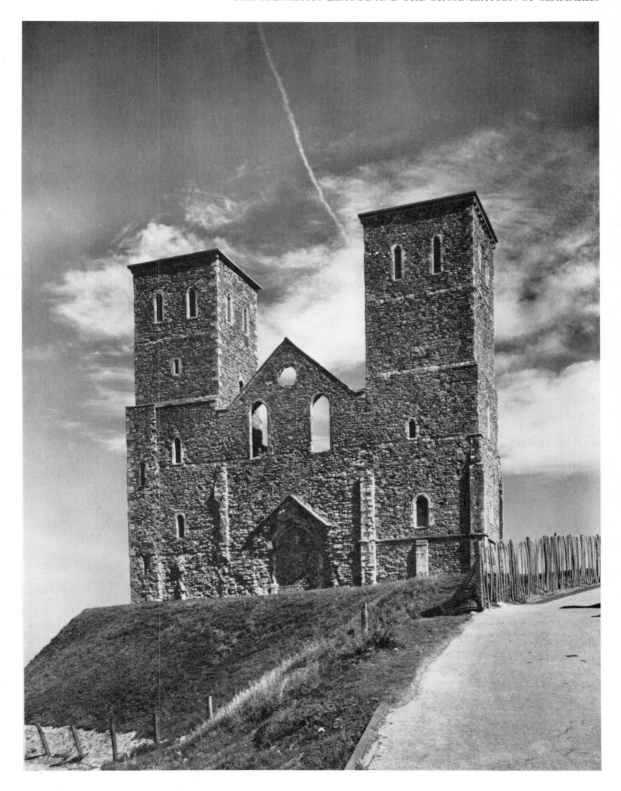

charitable origins, was beginning to assume the role of an 'academy' of nautical wisdom to which rulers looked for advice and in which a few well-educated men of science could sit comfortably alongside the hard-bitten sea captains who had been schooled only by survival in the dangerous sea. An instrument had been forged for training skilled and reliable pilots, and the ground was prepared for establishing fixed navigational aids where they found them most needed. Thus the English, coming late into the field of seamarking, were able to adapt rather than adopt the system of Bardze, Barsenmeister, Bakensteker and Tonnenleger, which had evolved in the North German rivers under the aegis of the Hanse. The methods of seamarking used in the complex sea-channels of the Low Countries must have been familiar to all experienced captains, and certainly the Brethren of Trinity House must have known something of the technology used in the manufacture of buoys, the protection and driving-in of beacon poles and the siting of artificial leading marks. The infra-structure was, however, lacking until well into the seventeenth century.

As the Hanseatic League began to break up under many stresses, among which were the trading competition from Dutch companies and the English merchant adventurers, the legacy it left of commercial and maritime probity, of sound methods of controlling piracy and cargo-theft, and of how to build and maintain useful seamarks was absorbed by the nations who controlled the narrow seas and the routes to the Atlantic.

Sources for Chapter III

J. Bailey
W. Behrmann
Crommelin and van Suchtelen
E. P. Edwards
C. G. Harris
H. Henningsen
A. W. Lang
H. J. Lutterman and K. Steinbach
K. Klessman
S. McGrail
H. O. Müller
E. G. R. Taylor
P. Thompson
D. W. Waters

IV

Beacons

The word beacon comes from the low German word '*Bake*'. Its meaning in Frisia and North Germany, from which many people emigrated to Britain, is a signal pole or construction placed in or near the water. The plural of Bake is Baken and it is this plural form which has come down to us as Beacon. The reason for the adoption of the plural form in England may well derive from the fact that it was customary for primitive surveyors to use two poles on the summits of hills to line up the ancient trackways (see Chapter I). A further clue comes from a survey map of the Sussex coast made for purposes of defence in 1587, the year before the Spanish Armada sailed up the English Channel, which shows a number of paired beacons sited either on headlands or near the entrances to small havens or boat-beaching places (known as staithes on the East Coast and stades in Sussex). The beacons are portrayed as narrow cones and look as if they were built of stone. Placed so near each other, they must have been used to make transit lines to fix position off a headland, avoid dangers or at the correct point of entry to a haven.

We know from other evidence that the English, particularly, used hill-top and cliff-top sites for signal fires and that the system of national defence required the local military lieutenant to see to it that men were employed to maintain stores of fuel at all these beacons. Since the sites usually coincided with those on which two surveying poles or two cairns had been set up, or on the coast where two permanent structures were maintained as transit lines for sailors at sea, we can readily understand why the English term derives from the plural of Bake. The English also have developed the word 'beacon' to mean a high point of land, or even the summit of a mountain, and the other connotation of a fire or light signal has brought yet another meaning into the language. There is no doubt, however, that the original meaning is a mark, made of either wood or stone, which is of use to the navigator and it is in this sense that it is used in this chapter.

As described earlier, the Romans built timber signal towers and also masonry beacon towers which, following the example of the Pharos tower, were for both military and navigational use. The history of such

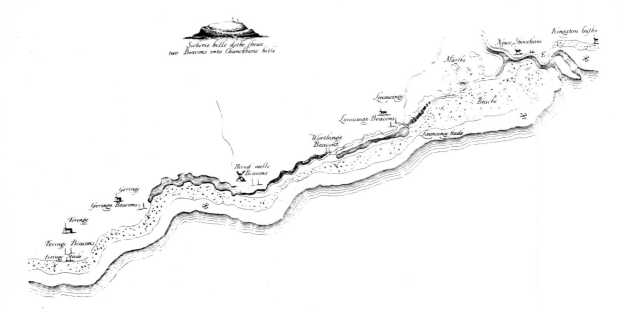

Coastal defence map of 1587. Six pairs of land beacons are shown on the stretch of Sussex coast between Littlehampton and Shoreham. Note also the twin beacons on the inland Sieberie Hille. (M. A. Lower, ed., A Survey of the Coast of Sussex, courtesy of West Sussex Records Office)

purpose-built fire towers is inextricably linked with the early history of beaconage, with coastal defence and with the communication of danger warnings. Their development mainly as navigational aids is described in Chapter VII.

The original German word *Bake*, meaning signal poles on or below the water line, derived from the no doubt much more ancient practice of driving tree branches into the mud along the low water mark of tidal estuaries or to show up shallows on rivers. In Northern Europe birch branches were most frequently used because their stems were long and strong enough to penetrate the ground and the plume of twigs was conspicuous enough to be seen from a distance. These primitive channel markers are still used throughout Europe where soft mud and a minimum of wave action make them reliable.

In the Venetian lagoons massive timber tripods have been used as seamarks for more than a thousand years. For deeper waters with a hard shingly bottom, strong tidal currents and considerable wave action, stouter poles are required. Shallow draft vessels would be necessary to drive in heavy poles: such barges (Bardzen) would have been equipped with tripod lifting gear and a pile-driver of stone or metal. The longer and sturdier baken often had pointed iron shoes to ease their penetration into the ground. In exposed waterways they were designed to extend 3m above high water. By the thirteenth century there were probably already quite sophisticated arrangements for the preparation, fixing, replacement and moving of beacon poles. The fact that the Rialto of Venice was built on a mudbank consolidated with thousands of vertical piles shows that in medieval times there was already a considerable store of knowledge about the driving of poles into the seabed. German records suggest that at least three men were needed to drive in the standard kopfbaken.

Another method of fixing a beacon pole on a hard foreshore or stony shoal was to place a pole in a half barrel, then fill the barrel with stones, and finally surround the whole structure with a mound of boulders. We learn from the records of Trinity House at Kingston-upon-Hull that this method was used, but it cannot have been very efficient unless the foundation was very firm and unless cement was used to prevent the stones from being dislodged and undermined by tide and wave action.

One of the problems of entering a river estuary on a full tide is to know whether the marks are on the left or right side of the channel. In a curving channel, and few channels are straight, the right and left hand markers may, on approach, be seen as a confused jumble. A bundle of birch twigs or a willow basket could be tied to the top of the poles in order to indicate one side of the channel, the opposite side having just bare poles. The sailor would have to possess local knowledge to understand the usage. In the Baltic and the Gulf of Bothnia where there were tideless conditions, winding channels and shallow water, and where there was often no natural indication of upstream and downstream, or tidal flow was complicated, a convention was established that birch branch bundles with their stems upwards denoted the southerly side of the channel, while those with their stems down and twigs up denoted the northerly side. We do not know when colour was first used to indicate laterality, but red poles proved in time to be the best contrast with the black tarred or unpainted ones.

The Bremer Bake, built on a half-tide shoal in the outer approaches to the River Weser. The picture dates from about 1790. Note the construction of timber on a rock foundation. It was often rebuilt and improved until in 1850 it was replaced by the Hoheweg Lighthouse. (A. W. Lang, Geschichte des Seezeichenwesens*)*

As the channel markers moved farther down the rivers into open tideways and estuaries durability must have been a problem, and we know from illustrations that by the fourteenth century important channel bends were marked with taller strutted poles or tripods. The next stage was to erect more elaborate timber-framed constructions at the ends of submerged sandspits near the entrance of important deep-water channels. These were designed to withstand storms and the undermining action of shifting sands, and they also had to have sufficient height and singularity of silhouette to make them recognizable from afar by incoming ships. These structures, when large enough, came to be known as Kapen (see Chapter VI). They were costly to build and maintain and were considered beyond the resources of the local Barsenmeister: special capital sums had to be voted by the harbour authorities for their erection.

The English, perhaps due to the geological features of much of their coastline, or perhaps due to legal uncertainties in Tudor times, seem to have relied more on land than marine seamarks. Though the Act of 1566 entitled the Trinity House to erect 'beacons, markes and signes of the sea', it did not specifically permit placing them in the water. This was probably still the prerogative of the Lord High Admiral, and though the Elizabethan holders of that office appear to have taken few initiatives in seamarking Trinity House had to be careful not to offend such important political figures. Thus we find that it was the decay of Margate Steeple, 'a marke or signe of the sea' according to the Act, which was used as the excuse for marking the Narrows near Reculver in the Thames Estuary. The initiative almost certainly came from Trinity House or the Cinque Ports, whose pilots would have been constantly exposed to the dangers of shipwreck on those exposed shoals. As a beacon erected on a sandbank did not prove durable, the passage was buoyed and remained buoyed well before the Act of 1593 finally gave Trinity House absolute authority and responsibility for marking the Thames Estuary.

Where a coastline was rocky and presented a confusing profusion of cliffs, headlands and islands, it was appropriate to build a cairn of stones or even a well jointed pyramidal or cylindrical tower to indicate the entrance to a sheltered fjord. Such stone towers were built on the coast of Norway by the Vikings, and by the Romans and their successors in Spain and France. The nature of the Channel and Atlantic coasts of Brittany is such that the building of stone towers was begun early.

Monasteries, such as that of St Mathieu near Ushant which commanded the approaches to Brest and Camaret, were built on clifftops and concerned themselves not only with the rescue and comfort of the shipwrecked, but the salvage of wreck goods, pilotage and possibly the erection of seamarks, profits from salvage and pilotage no doubt paying for the others.

Guilds of mariners and pilots were often formed under ecclesiastical guidance and protection. It is believed that the original Guild of the Holy Trinity, the forerunner of the Trinity House Corporation of

Dartmouth daymark, built in 1864 by the Dartmouth Harbour Commissioners and 80ft tall. It is on a high point of land between Dartmouth and Brixham and in good visibility can be seen from about 25 miles out to sea. (P. Hassell)

Deptford Strond, was set up under the administration of Stephen Langton, the great archbishop-statesman of Canterbury in the twelfth century. The guild was empowered not only to care for the dependants of dead or sick sailors, but to assist in pilotage, to provide seamarks, to teach navigation, to salvage cargoes and to exact tolls and Customs on behalf of the Archbishopric.

The history of the Trinity Guild of Kingston-upon-Hull, of which full records are available, throws light on the way in which such guilds were founded in medieval times and how they gradually came to be responsible for seamarking. The Guild or Fraternity of Masters, Pilots

and Seamen of the Trinity House of Kingston-upon-Hull was founded
in 1369, seventy years after that walled town had been granted a Royal
Charter by King Edward I. By 1369 Kingston had a population of
about 2,000. Forty-nine men and women were the founding members
of the Guild of Holy Trinity, which was concerned chiefly with
religious observances, the saying of masses for the souls of the dead, and
charitable support of Brethren who had fallen on hard times. The
document setting out the rules of the guild was written in Latin: it
stipulated a membership subscription of two shillings annually and
gave a list of fines, to be paid in so many pounds of wax, for ill
behaviour or breaking the rules of the fraternity. (Wax was a valuable
commodity and easily saleable.) By 1398 a second subscription deed
showed a membership of 250, from all walks of life but mainly those
connected with the sea. In 1456, when the third subscription deed was
drawn up, we get a glimpse of the financial machinery behind the
guild's activities. Twenty-four shipmaster Brethren agreed to pay a
proportion of the 'lowage and stowage' money into the guild's funds.
Lowage and stowage, which came to be known as primage in the
following year when King Henry VI granted a charter to the guild
authorizing the collection of this money for the benefit of its charities,
was an impost levied on the loading and unloading of cargo in the port.

The English shipmasters using the port came to expect something for
their money, and in later years their demands crystallized into
sanctions against those shipping cargo in foreign vessels if an English
ship was available, the licensing of pilots with penalties for using
unlicensed ones, and the provision of navigational aids. The charitable
functions of the guild were directed especially to the care of distressed
seamen of all nationalities, the compensation of the victims of piracy
and the provision of support for sea-widows and orphans. The Charter
of 1585 gave the Brethren the right to establish beacons and buoys in
the River Humber and to levy charges on all shipping in the river, but
they had already established at least one beacon before that: from 1567
onwards, there are various references to the repair of a wooden beacon
at Paull a few miles east of Kingston. The Lord High Admiral in 1585,
the year of Elizabeth's charter, wrote in his preamble, 'The Trinity
House of Kingston-upon-Hull, for the better conduct, safeguard and
passing of ships in and out of the River Humber, have already placed
and made one buoy in the said river and are presently to erect, make,
set up, keep, have and maintain two other buoys and two beacons in
the same river to their great expense and charge and request to me by
Robert Bate on their behalf for levying some reasonable portion of
every ship and vessel passing into the said river of Humber towards
defraying of charges which they have been at and hereafter shall be in
erecting, keeping and maintaining of the said beacons and buoys in the
said river Humber.' A wordy statement, no doubt, but one which led to
the Queen authorizing a toll of sixpence per ton for alien ships of
greater than 60 tons burden and fourpence for those between 30 and
60 tons, English ships to be charged at half rate. Inward pilotage was to
cost 6s 8d and outward pilotage 20s. In 1597, money taxed for

Padstow Daymark. Typical Cornish daymark of local stone, 40ft tall. (D. B. Hague)

'buoyage and beaconage' was separated from the original Primage tax. We can therefore see from the Hull records how the seamarking of a difficult tidal river came to be undertaken by a guild founded originally for religious and charitable purposes. We learn also of the great difficulties they had in making and keeping a wooden beacon in situ. It appears from their accounts that the beacon was constantly being repaired or replaced. (Buoys, or cannes as they were then known in England, were ultimately found to be more economical in the rough conditions of the Humber.)

Thus, whereas in the Baltic, North Germany and Flanders the installation and maintenance of beacons was largely the responsibility of the free cities of the Hanse, the provision of fixed seamarks was in England and France often entrusted to the great ecclesiastical foundations, or to the Trinity Guilds formed under church patronage. In Elizabethan times, the charts of Burroughs and Norman show that during her reign there was a gradual switch from beacons to buoys in the Thames Estuary, presumably because the former had not proved durable. At the end of the sixteenth century there were no more than four beacons and five buoys in the whole Estuary; by 1818 there were seventy-three buoys.

Monasteries and abbeys were often conveniently in prominent situations on headlands where they could be used as seamarks; and hermits, who lived in isolated places sometimes near the entrances of havens, tried to help mariners. Thus, in 1349 a petition was made to the Bishop of Norwich on behalf of a hermit, John Puttock, who lived in a shelter on the bishop's marsh near Lynn. This man had erected a high cross for the benefit of sailors navigating the Wash.

The entrances to both Lynn and Boston in the Wash were marked by pole beacons from an early date, but we do not know how they were

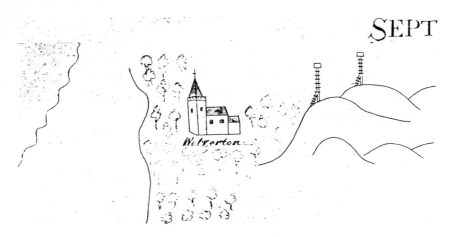

SEPT

Part of a pre-Armada map of the Chase of Rising just northeast of Kings Lynn, showing twin beacon poles on a hill between Wolverton Church and Sandringham. They are equipped for climbing and may have sometimes been lit. (Norfolk Records Office)

maintained and financed. Both ports, which were very important in medieval times, had strong Hanseatic links and it is likely that their burghers set up some organization similar to those of Hamburg, Bremen and Emden, but all early records have been lost. A chart of Lynn entrance in the sixteenth century shows two beacons on a hill near Wolverton which appear to have been used as leading marks and to have been equipped with fire-braziers. Elizabeth's Charter of 1572 to the town of Boston mentions beacons in a state of decay and instructs the burghers to put them in order. By 1693, Greenvile Collins' charts show eight pole beacons and eight buoys in the approaches to Lynn, and four buoys and twelve pole beacons in the Boston Deeps.

With the great expansion of sea trade in the sixteenth and seventeenth centuries and the increasingly successful suppression of piracy in European waters, timber beacons and beacon towers became more sophisticated and began to tax the engineering skills of resourceful people in England and Holland. Maps and charts show that there were in 1600 over twenty beacon towers of wood or stone marking the coasts of Southeast England. The survey maps of the Sussex coast made in 1587 show that, in addition to frequent twin beacons used for transit bearings, there were other round buildings on promontories, subscribed e.g. 'this Donehouse is a marck at sea'. The origin of the word 'donehouse' is uncertain. Greenvile Collins' survey of 1682–93 shows that substantial pole beacons with tripod legs were favoured to mark obstructions near British harbour entrances (see Chapter VI). There were two such beacons at the Whittaker Sands marking the northwestern side of the King's Channel and the Swin leading through to the inner Thames.

A large tripod beacon on Black Rock, north of the Wirral Peninsula, was Liverpool's sole fixed navigational aid. The important drying harbour of Leith also had only one similar mark. Aberdeen and Tynemouth each had a tripod beacon marking the edge of the low water line near their entrances, whereas Blythe had no less than three beacons marking the limits of drying shoals. Sunderland had two beacons, and both Lynn and Boston had many pole beacons outlining

Elizabethan map of Selsey Bill showing the entrances to Chichester and Pagham havens. Three pairs of twin beacons are shown, though their orientation may not be accurate as the map was drawn for purpose of defence against the Spanish Armada. Two 'Donehouses' are used as 'Marckes at Sea'. (M. A. Lower, ed., A Survey of the Coast of Sussex, *courtesy of West Sussex Records Office)*

the inner channels. Falmouth Rock, a half-tide rock in the fairway southeast of Pendennis Head, had a beacon placed on it to make it conspicuous at all states of the tide, and the Rectors of Falmouth were empowered by Act of Parliament to collect a toll of sixpence from each ship entering Falmouth to pay for the maintenance of this beacon. Towers known as *balises* were also built on many half-tide rocks in Brittany. An attempt was made to build a 30ft high beacon on the Wolf Rock off Land's End in the early nineteenth century, but although the enterprise was carefully planned and cost £12,000 the beacon did not survive the first winter.

Trinity House, Hull, maintained several landfall beacons on the shore to the north and south of the Humber River entrance and there are regular references throughout the eighteenth and nineteenth centuries to their repair. Donna Nook beacon had to have new foundations in 1852 and at the same time its height was increased to 65ft. Landfall beacons on the East Coast of England generally resembled the Frisian kapen in design (see Chapter VI), and were frequently of lattice construction and had easily recognized topmarks shaped like a triangle, ball, diamond or perhaps a brandrith (an iron grating used as a fire-base). They were usually sited not as leading marks for a channel but as clearing marks for offshore shoals when kept 'open of' (not directly in line with) some prominent landmark. The beacon on the Naze Headland south of Harwich was a substantial masonry tower, while the one at Felixstowe was of lattice type.

In the eighteenth and nineteenth centuries a great number of masonry beacons, single and much taller than their sixteenth century equivalents, were built on remote headlands and islands as daymarks.

Ruff Reef beacon in the Orkneys, dating from 1840 and replacing an older and less durable beacon. A good example of early ironwork. (R. W. Munro, Scottish Lighthouses*)*

They were designed as recognition marks capable of being identified from far out to sea and were often very tall (up to 100ft) and had distinctive shapes and perhaps colours. Some were castellated, others conical or tapering, and some were three-sided. The earliest of these was at St Martin's, the most northerly island of the Scillies, and one of the most prominent was on Gribbin Head in South Cornwall. A beacon tower built on the Roches Duon off Roscoff in Brittany in 1791 was provided with a shelter for shipwrecked sailors which still exists.

Beacons were also sometimes built by naval surveyors who were seeking to chart coasts and formidable dangers in far distant seas. Thus Blackwood, who had been entrusted with the difficult task of finding a safe channel through the Great Barrier Reef to the Torres Strait north of Australia, located a gap in the reef near Raine Island. Obtaining a work force of twenty ex-convict masons and carpenters from the governor of New South Wales, he set about quarrying coral block and erected a beacon on the island in four months which stood 40ft above sea level and was 30ft in circumference. It had three wooden floors, a rainwater catchment and storage tank, and contained emergency supplies for castaways.

The tripod beacon, which later came to be known in English as a dolphin, had its legs driven deep into the seabed by pile drivers. Later, the Mitchell screw pile, invented in 1832, was used to sink the legs of

The prominent St Martin's daymark, Isles of Scilly, built in the late seventeenth century and the oldest known stone seamark in Britain.

more elaborate iron structures even farther into the ground. By the nineteenth century, concrete foundations were laid within cylindrical caissons whenever the bedrock could be reached. An early example of this method was the iron beacon built on the Shingle Sands off Reculver. With such a deep and secure foundation, the top structure could be built either of granite blocks or of metal lattices. By the twentieth century, the use of sophisticated caissons, powerful pumps and deep-sea divers enabled many such structures to be built. Many in important positions were provided with some form of automatic lighting, either gas-fuelled or electrical where marine cables could be laid.

Modern caisson-built sea beacon in German waters. Note wind generator for automatic light. (F-K. Zemke)

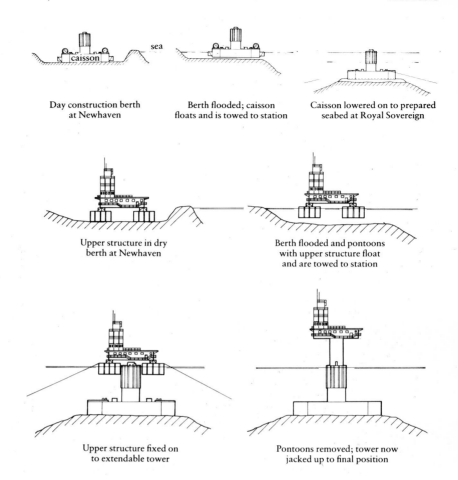

Royal Sovereign Light Tower built on a shoal and replacing a lightship. (Trinity House)

Construction stages of the Royal Sovereign Lighthouse. After the upper module was centred over the base and tower it was secured by concreting. The inner tower was then raised hydraulically to lift module and light structure clear of the waves. Sir Wm. Halcrow & Partners were the designers. (K. Sutton-Jones, Pharos)

Day construction berth at Newhaven

Berth flooded; caisson floats and is towed to station

Caisson lowered on to prepared seabed at Royal Sovereign

Upper structure in dry berth at Newhaven

Berth flooded and pontoons with upper structure float and are towed to station

Upper structure fixed on to extendable tower

Pontoons removed; tower now jacked up to final position

In recent times the technology which has enabled offshore oilrigs to be fixed to the seabed has been used to convert some floating seamarks into fixed structures. Generally, it is better for a lighted mark to be fixed rather than floating as the vertical spread of the light need not be so great as it has to be from a buoy rocking and heeling in a tideway. The narrower beam requires less power for a given intensity of light and thus the gas cylinders or batteries need to be replenished less often.

Several ways of fixing minor lights to the seabed have been developed. The simplest method in shallow water is to have a moulded Resinex floating beacon shackled by a swivel onto a heavy concrete block on the seabed. The tubular beacon is tall enough to take up the tidal range. In deeper, stormier conditions a base has to be prepared by underwater teams and then a prefabricated gantry or tower is floated out to the site, sunk and fixed to it. The Swedish engineer Robert Gellerstad developed the so-called 'telescopic lighthouse' which, after being floated out to its base, sunk, fixed and filled with ballast, could then be jacked up hydraulically to its required height. The English Royal Sovereign light and meteorological station, which has replaced a lightship, was built ashore in two sections which were floated out to the prepared site in succession. The Irish Kish Bank Lighthouse, which also replaced a lightship and was built ashore, was towed into position in 1965 and went into service almost immediately.

Several American platform lights have been built on exactly the same principles as oilrig platforms, while the English Inner Dowsing Light is actually a converted drilling rig. The Dutch Goeree (pronounced hooray) light platform and weather station is familiar to those who listen to the Shipping Forecasts. These seabed structures, though so strange and modernistic in shape and though functioning as complex lighthouses, can yet be linked through a thousand years of history to the pole beacon and birch branch of the past.

Sources for Chapter IV

J. Bailey
G. Collins
E. P. Edwards
D. S. Hague and R. Christie
C. G. Harris
A. W. Lang
M. A. Lower
R. Morcken
G. S. Ritchie
A. Storey
K. Sutton-Jones
P. Thompson

V
Buoys

The first use of buoys was probably to mark abandoned anchors or fixed moorings. Exactly when the principle of a visible, floating, but fixed object was adapted for channel marking is unknown, but the first written evidence was in an early medieval seamen's manual *La Compasso da Navigare* (1295), which gives sailing directions for the Mediterranean and the Iberian coast up to Cape St Vincent, and which refers to buoys within the Guadalquivir River in the approaches to Sevilla. In Northern Europe, there are early medieval references to buoys within the entrance to the great River Maas which carries most of the waters of the Rhine and Meuse to the North Sea.

Clearly, the need for buoys was chiefly in those places where the depth of water, the strength of the stream, and the variability of deep-water channels precluded the use of fixed beacons or land marks. This is why they were first used just within the mouths of great rivers which were discharging large volumes of water. Although floating beams or timber rafts anchored by ropes to the seabed were probably first used as anchor buoys or navigational marks, they would have soon lost their flotation and have had to be replaced frequently. The probability is, though, that simple timber floats were used well within the shelter of rivers throughout Europe from an early date. Such floats would have been inadequate for the strong currents of the big river estuaries, however, which is just where they would be most needed to guide the larger ships of the twelfth and thirteenth centuries. What was needed was a longer-lasting buoy with more flotation.

One of the first reliable records of air-containing barrel buoys dates from 1358 in the Maasgat (otherwise known as the Maas Sluis or Maasmond) which is in the area now occupied by the city of Rotterdam. A little earlier, in 1323, there is mention in an old document of the need for buoyage in the Vlie and the Marsdiep, the northern and northwestern channels leading to the Zuider Zee and the important trading centres of Amsterdam and Kampen. Throughout the fifteenth century there were difficulties between these two towns as to their responsibility for buoyage and beaconage in the Marsdiep and their right to retain the resulting Tonnengeld; Philip of Burgundy and the rulers of the Island of Texel took a part in these administrative controversies. The route from the Marsdiep through the Texel Stroom and from the Vlie into the shallow Zuider Zee was very important to Amsterdam, Kampen and Enkhuizen, and there is evidence that wherever possible pole beacons were used. Tonnen were used in the deeper water. By the time that Wagenhaer's and Blaeu's charts were published at the end of the sixteenth century, there were 43 buoys laid in the Zuider Zee and its approaches, 27 in the North German rivers, but only 17 in England (Terrel). In 1777 Trinity House was maintaining 21 buoys in the Thames Estuary, and by 1818 the number had grown to 73 there and in its approaches.

If a simple wine or beer cask were to be used as a buoy, there would be a problem in securing the mooring chain to the belly of the barrel. It would have been difficult to insert a strong enough mooring ring through the staves without weakening the whole structure and causing leaks. Thus, the mooring buoys were called by the same name as a barrel, a tonne, and though those responsible for laying them were known as tonnenlegers or barrel-layers, the design of the marine buoy soon became fundamentally different from that of barrels. The simple idea which evolved was to narrow one end so that it could be closed by a stout oaken plug through which the mooring ring could be secured. The fassbinders or barrel makers of the Netherlands and North Germany learnt to shape the oak staves in such a way that each was triangular in shape with a blunt apex of about 1in width. The outer face of the triangular stave would be anything up to 6in wide; the opposing surfaces of the staves would be carefully planed or spokeshaved at the correct angle so that each stave would fit snugly with its neighbour. Thirty or more would be required to make a good cone-shaped buoy. The hollow apex was filled by a conical wooden

Typical conical Seetonnen (barrel buoys) lying in the Hamburg buoy yard in 1675. There is a strongly fixed mooring ring at the apex of the cone and the Hamburg City emblem is carved on the base. (A. W. Lang, Geschichte des Seezeichenwesens)

plug through which an iron mooring ring had previously been secured. The apices of the staves were carefully moulded round the plug and all surfaces treated with tar to achieve a watertight seal. Then a heated iron hoop was hammered around the ends of the staves enclosing the plug and as it cooled and contracted it sealed all joints firmly. Further hoops of increasing diameter, perhaps ten or twelve in all, were hammered round the staves to bring them together until all that was left was the rabbeting in of strong oak boards, suitably shaped to close the base of the cone, and the fixing of the final and widest iron hoop. These end planks had to be immensely strong and well made; in later

A wooden nun buoy of about 1790. The key-shaped topmark indicates ownership by the City of Bremen, which was responsible for buoyage of the Weser. The nun buoy, which is a double cone, developed from the old single conical buoy. (A. W. Lang, Geschichte des Seezeichenwesens*)*

times they were often carved or decorated with the insignia of the port to which they belonged.

The Dutch first developed a method of testing newly completed tonnes for watertightness. In Brielle, a small town south of the Maas Sluis and close to the present Rotterdam Europort, they invented a method involving air pressure from bellows. A small hole was bored through the tonne, air was blown in and all seams checked for leaks. If the tonne was leaky, it was filled with water to see whether swelling of the timber would close the previously marked leaks. Only if the tonne was completely watertight and well tarred was it passed for service. Such a tonne, measuring up to 10ft long and 5ft maximum diameter, was expected to give good service for ten years; without tar, it would not last three years.

The tonne, so carefully constructed, sealed and painted with pitch and tar, was ready to be moored with its apex below water and its broad flat base upwards. From the illustrations it is apparent that tonnes of this design would be both weighty and strong. The method of securing the mooring ring to the strongest part of the tonne made them capable of withstanding the tugging and chafing which would have been made inevitable in the choppy waters of tidal estuaries. All the early manuals of navigation and the first crude charts of river entrances in Northern Europe show tonnes of conical barrel construction, so the design must have proved durable. In more sheltered waters, especially in England at a later date, horizontal barrel buoys were still used, despite their vulnerability to wear and tear; they were known as cask buoys.

According to Lang, the tonne's mooring chain had long loose links and swivels at the top and bottom ends. The lower swivel was shackled or joined to a strong iron ring which had been fashioned from a

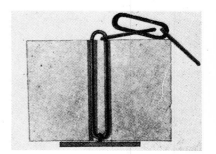

Hand-worked stone sinker for an Ems buoy of about 1810. The mooring chain runs through the central hole. (A. W. Lang, Geschichte des Seezeichenwesens*)*

wrought-iron rod bent back on itself like a split pin. The two split ends then passed through a central hole in a large worked stone of rectangular shape and were either splayed out in the under surface of the stone or attached to a strong iron plate there. An alternative design was to encircle the stone by a tight chain in a cut groove and then to shackle the mooring chain onto this. Disused millstones were often used in England for mooring buoys, but by the sixteenth century specially fashioned sinkers were exported from Yorkshire quarries.

One problem was theft, the thieves often claiming a fee for 'finding' the tonne adrift! Brass locks were designed to foil removal.

The first record in Germany of a specialized vessel for buoy-laying, a Tonnenschiff, is from Hamburg in 1460, though it is probable that the Dutch and Flemish had developed such vessels first. A little later, Emden had a specially designed, copper-sheathed Tonnenschiff of 30 tons burden and a crew of more than ten men. Not until 1745 was there a reference to the Trinity House sloop being sent to clean the buoys in the southern approaches to the Thames. A special buoy yacht was not commissioned in the Humber until 1783.

Winter ice in German and Dutch waters had, by the seventeenth century, caused the authorities controlling the Weser and Elbe to lift the heavy tonnes in November and replace them with light flag buoys for the winter season. This practice probably continued until the wooden tonnes were superseded in the nineteenth century.

In England, we cannot be sure when the barrel construction was first adopted. The custom up to Tudor times was for the Lord High Admiral to be responsible for appointing agents in the larger ports to mark the seaways and although this could be an office of profit both for the Admiral and his agents, who were empowered to levy tolls on cargo, there is no evidence of any systematic laying of buoys. In 1503, there is a reference to buoys to be provided for Sandwich Harbour, but there is no information as to their construction and no surviving illustrations. The drawing of charts was not usual at that time. Later sixteenth century charts show no buoys outside Sandwich, but just one pole beacon. The 1514 charter enabling the Master and Brethren of Trinity House of Deptford to collect some of the tolls from ships using the harbours of the Thames Estuary provided a big stimulus, not only to the laying of buoys but also to finding the best methods of construction and maintenance. One of Henry's most trusted mariners, Thomas Spert, for a time Captain of the *Mary Rose*, was made Trinity House's first Master, and no doubt he was aware of all the development work which had been done in the Netherlands. However, it was not until 1593, in the reign of Queen Elizabeth, that Lord High Admiral Effingham finally surrendered the right to collect tolls for seamarks and thus gave Trinity House a secure source of income. Rutters published later in Elizabeth's reign, including translations from Dutch, show tonnes of continental design in English waters.

From being backward in the business of seamarking, the English gradually advanced until, by the nineteenth century, they had become leaders in the field. This was in large measure due to the growing power and efficiency of the various Trinity Houses and also to the great expansion of English sea trading which followed the opening up of routes to the Americas and the Indian Ocean. Geographically, England and Scotland were in a good position to exploit that trade, and after the defeat of Spain's sea power in 1588 English merchant adventurers had enormous opportunities not only overseas but in Flanders, North Germany and the Baltic. The parallel growth of Dutch mercantile and naval power after the sea defeat of Spain led to the exchange of ideas on shipbuilding and navigation, but also to rivalry which culminated in the Anglo-Dutch wars of the seventeenth century.

The Trinity House of Hull had existed for two hundred years before it was granted a charter in 1585 by Elizabeth I. This entitled it to collect dues for seamarking, but they had had great difficulty in designing and mooring suitable buoys in the Humber estuary. Their records indicate that at the time of the charter they were maintaining one wooden canne (as buoys were called in England until the end of the sixteenth century) off the Den Sand west of Spurn Point. We know that iron was used in its construction as there are records of payments to a blacksmith; other items purchased included nails, pitch, lead, hoops, stone and chain. The buoy seems to have been frequently out of service or out of position as there were payments to mooring crews and for repairs and recaulking. In 1621 the Brethren bought a ready-made buoy from Holland for £11 9s 4d, which tells us something of the relatively advanced state of Dutch buoyage.

Later in the seventeenth century a second buoy was moored off Cleeness Sands and after ineffectual and expensive attempts to erect a storm-proof beacon off the Burcom Sand north of Grimsby the Brethren moored another buoy there. These two buoys are the only ones shown within the Humber on Collins' chart based on a survey at the end of the century. The Brethren continued to have great difficulty in maintaining the buoys, which were frequently found adrift or waterlogged. When a buoy was brought back to the House at Hull for repairs, it is recorded that the tar was first scraped off, the buoy drained of water and dried, damaged wood and seams made good and the interior stuffed with peat, turves and rope ends, presumably in the hope that if the buoy again became waterlogged these low-density materials would help to keep it afloat. It seems that their ingenuity was in advance of their knowledge of physics. Old millstones were commonly used as sinkers. Evidently domestic techniques did not improve, for in 1682 another buoy was imported from Hamburg at a cost of £13 8s.

Collins' charts of 1693 show no less than eight tonne-type buoys in the entrances to Lynn and four to mark the banks enclosing the Boston Deeps, so that the Wash must at that time have been the most heavily buoyed area of Britain. Blakeney in North Norfolk was also well buoyed, and there were two buoys in the River Tyne between Shields and Newcastle. Unfortunately, we do not know whether the buoys were locally made or imported from Germany. The funds for their purchase and maintenance were derived from tolls levied on ships using the harbours and roadsteads, the Crown having surrendered its rights to several towns in the sixteenth century.

The diaries of Samuel Pepys make it very clear that Trinity House of Deptford was at that time both active and powerful, having the enthusiastic support of King Charles II and his brother. Pepys was himself Master in 1776 and used his considerable administrative talents to put the Corporation on a sound financial basis. Seamarks of this era included not only buoys but pole beacons, stone towers, leading marks and, rarely, fire or light towers (*vide infra*). Although the techniques of buoy manufacture and laying could not advance much until the advent of metal construction, Trinity House appears to have overcome the main organizational problems in the seventeenth and eighteenth centuries.

At first they employed a local agent at Margate to maintain the buoys in the South Channel and another at Harwich for the northern channels, but the work was not well done. The first mention of a buoy yacht was in 1745 when a Mr Widgeon was ordered by the Board to 'go down in the Trinity Sloop to clean the buoys in the South Channel'. From 1786 onwards they also employed an agent at Great Yarmouth who attended to the buoys and lightships in that area. Depots and yards were set up where buoys could be built, repaired and maintained, no doubt on the same lines as the Tonnenhäuser of the Hanseatic towns. A buoy yard and a buoy yacht were commissioned at Hull in 1783. Buoy yachts and later steam vessels were built with special equipment for raising and laying, and the inspection and repair of mooring chains. Most important, personnel were appointed locally to report the miscarriage of buoys, and skilled men were recruited for the buoy yachts and to replace or move marks which had gone adrift or been shifted by storms. Such centres were in Harwich, Hull, Newcastle, Deptford, Great Yarmouth and Ramsgate.

Greenvile Collins' charts and sailing directions, compiled after his coastal survey of both kingdoms in 1682–93, show remarkably few buoys around the English coast, although they were used more extensively within rivers. For the western ports, the only one was at Dublin bar. In the Thames approaches the only buoys Collins recorded were a bunch of five in the narrows leading to the Kentish Flats, north of Reculver church. This shallow passage between Margate Roads and the main river was a major problem for Thames pilots. There was another buoy by the Red Sand off Sheppey, and an important buoy to mark the shallow Spitts passage between the Wallet and the King's Channel southwest of the Gunfleet Sand and east of Frinton. There was another at the north end of the Gunfleet marking Goldersmore's Gat, a safe deep-water passage through to The Naze headland and to Harwich just north of it. A buoy is also shown moored at the southern tip of the extensive St Nicholas and Knowle Sands which enclose the Great Yarmouth Roads. The passage south of this buoy led northwest into the Roads and was known as St Nicholas' Gat. There were buoys and pole beacons in the close approaches to Lynn and Boston, on the Wash, maintained by the port authorities.

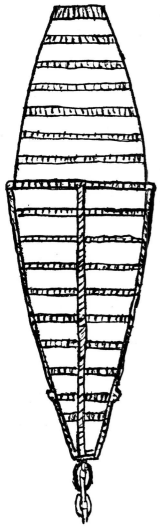

Typical eighteenth century nun buoy supplied by Messrs Bailey of Dundee to Trinity House of Kingston-upon-Hull in the early nineteenth century. (A. Storey)

There was great difficulty in keeping Humber buoys on station and in repair. The services of cooper and blacksmith were often needed, and many sailing ships collided with buoys and cast them adrift. Although there were the two buoys in the Humber, many other middle-ground banks in the Humber, the Solent and Southampton Water were unmarked. There were, however, two important buoys in the approaches to Spithead and Portsmouth, one marking the edge of the Horse Sand to the north and the other No Man's Sand to the south of the main channel, both occupying the positions of the existing nineteenth century circular forts.

Surveys of the Thames Estuary by Mackenzie and Spence during the eighteenth century led to the discovery of the Queen's Channel, which carried a least depth of 16ft and was an improvement on the earlier southern route over the Kentish Flats to Margate Roads. This channel was subsequently buoyed by Trinity House, and became the main entrance to the Port of London and the River Medway for vessels from France, Flanders and the English Channel.

The organization of Tonnenhaus, Tonnenschiff and Tonnenleger, with or without the supervisory Barsenmeister, which had been adopted by the Hanseatic towns and which was described earlier, remained the dominant one in North Europe throughout the seventeenth and eighteenth centuries. Arrangements based on Trinity House Corporations enabled the English, during the eighteenth century, to copy the best practices of North Europe and to pave the way for the advances of the nineteenth. The building of stone towers and lighthouses on the rocky Atlantic coasts of Britain and France, using the new methods of building pioneered by Winstanley, Rudyerd, Smeaton and others, tapped new sources of money and stimulated the

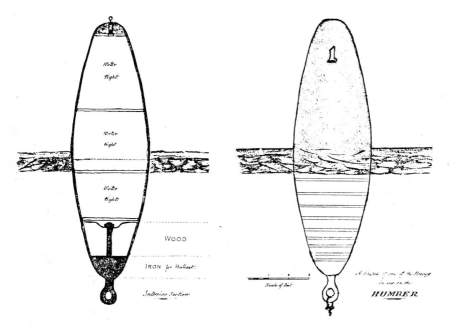

Wood and iron nun buoy of 1868, as used in the River Humber; one of a great variety of types manufactured before steel buoys came into common use. (A. Storey)

English to experiment with better methods of seamarking, but the drawbacks of wood for buoys prevented significant progress. In 1837 the buoys in the Humber were mainly nun buoys, constructed as double cones on the same principles as the original conical buoy of staves bound by iron loops. In 1848 a steam chest was installed for moulding the staves. However, by 1885 many all-iron buoys were being ordered by the Hull Trinity House.

It was the development of iron foundries and metalworking technology, which had earlier made possible the railways and iron ships, that really paved the way for improvements. Completely watertight iron buoys with horizontal and vertical bulkheads could be laid in deep and stormy channels with some certainty of their remaining on station and intact. They were of rivetted wrought-iron or steel and weighed over three tons. Iron buoys were used for wreck marking some years before they were generally adopted for channels. There was an enormous increase in stationing buoys in the late nineteenth century following the invention of these new methods of construction, and the watertight internal bulkheads greatly increased the reliability and durability of these early metal buoys. More and more were needed as the drafts of ships increased so that even deep shoals became dangers.

Bell buoys came into service in 1860, and whistle buoys were first used in England in 1880. Both were, of course, helpful to the mariner in fog, or who was near a danger or making a landfall in poor visibility. The English used compressed gas cylinders to power their whistle

Drawing of one of the first gas-lit buoys used in the River Humber. (A. Storey)

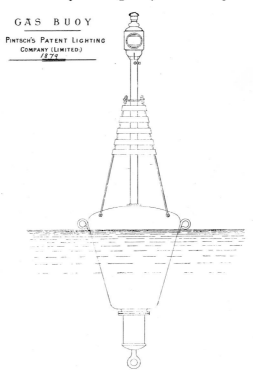

GAS BUOY

PINTSCH'S PATENT LIGHTING COMPANY (LIMITED.)
1879

buoys, but the French adopted an invention of M. Courtenay of New York which utlilised a column of seawater propelled upwards into the whistle tube by the rocking of the buoy, driving in front of it a volume of air which sounded the whistle. The resulting high-pitched moan can be heard for upwards of 3 miles in quiet conditions. The French also developed a taller form, the pillar or spar buoy, which could be seen at a greater distance than the more squat version favoured by Trinity House, although pillar buoys were recommended generally for seaways and landfalls by 1880 and are still so used today. High-focal-plane buoys require underwater tail tubes for stability, which can house the whistle tube apparatus.

The most important nineteenth century development of the metal buoy was the installation of lighting systems between 1879 and 1894. The power source in Pintsch's original German invention was compressed gas stored in a central reservoir or in packs of cylinders. Buoy lights were at first fixed (shown continuously), but as they could be mistaken for ships' lights, flashing or quick-flashing systems were later devised. Because of the need for an unattended, reliable flasher mechanism usable with gas, discontinuous lights appeared on buoys later than on lighthouses. Red flashing lights were also used; their range was not designed to exceed 3 miles at the most.

Although many beacons and fixed seamarks had recognizable topmarks from very early times – a barrel, willow basket, brush or crown – the conical wooden tonne was not well shaped for carrying a topmark. The carvings and decorations on its upper surface denoted ownership rather than a practical mark for recognition at any distance. The usefulness of topmarks on fixed beacons was very soon appreciated, and so the eighteenth century nun buoys, which were often 18ft long and constructed with a strong point at each end, usually carried a topmark. As metal buoys came into service, it was easy to incorporate a topmark on a iron lattice above the body of the buoy. The use of colours such as white, red, green and yellow also helped to identify particular buoys given local knowledge or adequate charts. However, there was no uniformity and the problems caused by different conventions of topmarking and colour led to many difficulties and confusions in the last hundred years. This will be described more fully in Chapter XI, but it is appropriate to remind the reader at this stage that the birch broom convention of the Baltic, which showed the north side of a channel by a downward pointed silhouette and the south side by an upward-pointing one, was later incorporated in most European systems of topmarking. To a nineteenth century sailor, 'point up' meant good water north of the mark, while 'point down' meant good water to the south. However, as an exception, an early chart of the entrance to the Maas Sluis shows that beacons with triangular points-up topmarks lined the north side of the low water line, while round topmarks lined the south side.

Despite these various confusions, it became fairly general in the nineteenth century for both Continental and British marks on the right-hand side leading into a port to have pointed tops and for those

An early metal bell buoy with a prominent basket topmark, 1886. (A. Storey)

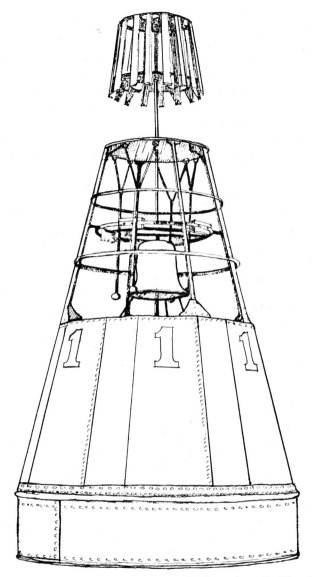

on the left-hand side to have flat tops (points down). The Liverpool area was a notable exception to this rule, but eventually conformed. For middle-ground shoals and mid-channel use, a round superstructure with painted horizontal bands and a round topmark became the convention. Buoys usually had their names or numbers painted on at least two sides: odd numbers were on the right and even on the left when coming in towards a harbour.

Cardinal topmarking developed where waters were non-tidal, channels intricate and not necessarily leading into a haven. The only evidence of systematic cardinal marking comes from late nineteenth century Russia, Sweden and Finland. Differentiation of the east and west sides of channels may be a later development.

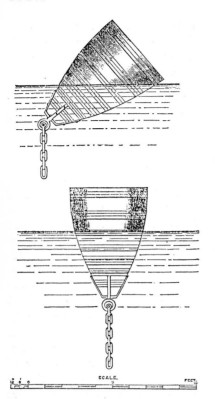

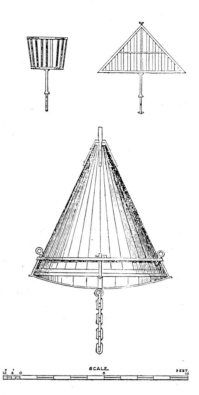

Some of the wide variety of buoys used in 1861. (From the Report of the Royal Commission of 1861)

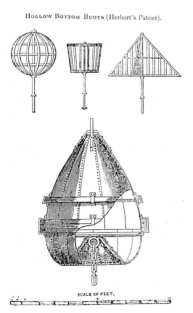

HOLLOW BOTTOM BUOYS (Herbert's Patent).

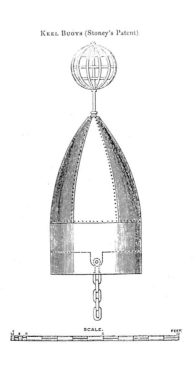

KEEL BUOYS (Stoney's Patent)

Although the colour in which iron buoys were painted was the subject of so much controversy during later years, early wooden buoys were mostly painted black and well tarred, though the use of white paint was widespread in many parts of Europe, especially for port-hand marks. Red paint was also sometimes used, but painted wooden buoys soon became foul so that the colour could not easily be seen.

After the invention of radar during the Second World War, many buoys were fitted with hexagonal radar reflectors.

THE MODERN BUOY

The typical metal buoy of today is composed of a large flotation chamber which is not divided into separate bulkheads but which, in the case of a lighted buoy, houses several gas cylinder 'pockets'. On the outer rim of the underwater surface of the buoy are two heavy steel lugs opposite each other. A chain bridle is shackled onto those and the mooring chain is shackled to a swivel on the mid-point of this bridle. If the buoy has an underwater tail tube the attachment of the mooring chain is necessarily more complex. The mooring is anchored by a flat sinker of appropriate weight. The chain is composed of 30m lengths and it is possible to replace a worn section when calibration of the links shows that wear has proceeded to a point of possible danger. Buoyage authorities regularly inspect and if necessary calibrate each section of mooring chain and keep records. Different authorities have different schedules for routine buoy inspection, chain calibration and repainting, but all require vessels powerful enough to lift the buoy, cable and sinker onto their decks. Trinity House keeps centralized records in its Harwich Depot of the state of all its buoys and beacons.

Beneath the central flotation chamber of the larger whistle or high focal plane buoys is bolted a long tail tube. If the tube does not house special apparatus but is there purely as ballast, it is filled with loose chain, the movement of which scours the inside of the tube. Above the central chamber is the superstructure, usually of metal latticework. Its height and shape varies with the buoy's function. At the apex of the superstructure is the lantern and its housing which may incorporate the radar reflector. Immediately above the lantern is the detachable topmark, which since the introduction of the IALA system all cardinal buoys carry (see Chapter XII).

All the separate components of the modern buoy are detachable and can be separately serviced and maintained. Within limits, parts are interchangeable so that a new lantern or a new lattice superstructure can be fitted onto an old, undamaged flotation chamber. This can be done at sea by the tender if a buoy has been damaged by collision. High-focal-plane buoys with long tail tubes are difficult to handle on the deck of the tender, so buoys of intermediate height are fitted with a circular skirt keel beneath the flotation chamber: this allows them to stand upright.

Smaller tubular spar buoys, often made of reinforced plastic, are today frequently moored in rivers and estuaries.

BUOY LIGHTING

Compressed oil gas was originally the favoured fuel, but about 1912 the inventive mind of Gustav Dalén of Sweden solved the problem of producing a flashing sequence by using acetylene gas pressure to activate a diaphragm valve beneath the gas jet. It was dangerous at that time to use acetylene and in one unfortunate experiment there was an explosion which blinded Dalén. While convalescing, he invented the Aga Stove and founded the Aga Company, now AB Pharos Marine, which is still a leading supplier of lighthouse equipment to the world. The brilliance of Dalén's gas-flow control system was recognized by the award of the Nobel Prize for Physics and its usefulness affirmed by its continued use today. A pilot light burns all the time and the main gas flow is emitted in a series of puffs to give the required sequence of flashes. The code of flashes is pre-set by screw adjustments of the diaphragm, its mounting and accessories.

The sun valve invented by Dalén and its more sophisticated photoelectric variants enable an automatic buoy or beacon gas light to be switched off at daybreak and on at dusk. The length of night use and the nature of the flash sequences determine the rate of gas consumption so that the authorities can calculate how often the gas cylinders need replacing. At every buoy service gas pressure in the cylinders is checked and those unable to give reliable service until the next relief are replaced.

After a way was found to stabilize acetylene gas by dissolving it in acetone retained in a porous mass containing charcoal, it became the cheapest and most reliable source of light power for buoys and minor lights. Nowadays the gas pressure can even be used to rotate a lightweight optic around the light source, but this additional use of the gas is not usually required for buoys but for larger floating lights or fixed beacons. It is remarkable that Dalén's ingenious use of acetylene in the early years of the century should still be of immense value in the modern world of sophisticated navigation aids. As so often with great inventions it is the beautiful simplicity of the concept and the sturdy reliability of its application which have stood the test of time.

New sources of power for buoy lighting are constantly being sought. Solar energy trapped by photovoltaic silicon panels to produce a charge for secondary batteries is one obvious source and some thirty years of research and development by various authorities, notably the French, are said to have overcome the main problems of wind and

Flash control gas valves for buoy lighting. (AB Pharos Marine Ltd)

weather corrosion. The silicon cells are embedded in a non-setting epoxy resin, sealed with rubber and protected by shatter-proof glass, and set at an angle of 60° to the horizontal round the circumference of the buoy. Electrical connections to the flash tube or rotating beacon light have to be protected against sea corrosion and it is in this area that problems are still being encountered. When they have been overcome and when the cost of the protected solar panels comes down to a point which makes solar power economically competitive with acetylene, we may expect a more general adoption of the system. At present it is being used both on buoys and fixed beacons at those sites where the replacement of gas cylinders entails exceptional expense or difficulty.

The second source of power which is being tapped on an experimental basis is wave action. When buoys are fitted with a tail tube, the air movement can drive a turbine which can charge batteries to energise the light. The Japanese system has an air turbine which can only use air flowing in one direction. As the air tube both sucks and blows, it has valves to direct the air in one direction. A recent innovation from Northern Ireland uses an air turbine which will generate power whichever way the air is flowing; this is called a Wells Turbine.

Sources for Chapter V

A. Ashley
W. J. Blaeu
Greenvile Collins
E. P. Edwards
C. G. Harris
A. W. Lang
G. S. Ritchie
A. Storey, (1) and (2)
E. G. R. Taylor
C. Terrell, personal communication
D. W. Waters
R. Woodman

VI

Leading Marks

(Range Marks)

Prominent towers, castles, windmills and churches have always been used in pilotage. Coastal recognition is an integral part of conducting a ship through difficult water and into sheltered anchorages and consequently churches and towers were often sited precisely to aid the coastal navigator. A prominent spire or mill can often be identified five miles out to sea.

Having recognized a familiar landmark, the mariner then needs directional information, which can be in the form of a second mark in the foreground on which to steer. If it were to be so situated that, kept in line with the larger landward mark, it led on a safe course between dangers on either hand, it would be treasured and memorised, for there is nothing more certain in navigation than a line between two known geographical points. Prominent above-water rocks used as leading marks might be painted white by sailors habitually using the harbour, but on a low island or point they would build a stone cairn or even a tower, then paint it white and surmount it with a cross, a barrel or a basket.

The use of such recognition and leading marks by sailors led to the more systematic marking of much-used channels and harbour entrances. The German word *Kape*, which was used for a wooden structure too large and complex to be referred to as a *Bake*, is no doubt derived from the Latin *caput*, *capa*, *caba* or *cape* meaning a headland. As headlands are so often a valuable recognition feature, many having their own peculiar silhouette or rock colour, it is possible to see how the same word came to be used for an artificial structure erected on some low-lying island, sandbank or half-tide rock. Certainly, the nature of the low North European coastline demanded such man-made structures, while the western Atlantic coasts were more plentifully provided with unique, prominent geological features. As described in Chapter IV, the use of pairs of beacons on headlands or near haven entrances was an established practice on the South Coast of England in Queen Elizabeth's reign. The way they are drawn on the map, and their twinning, indicates that they were man-made, probably of stone, and that despite being called beacons they were used as transit marks.

Steenbake and front leading mark at the mouth of the River Maas in 1665, from an engraving by Joost van Geel. Built and repeatedly repaired by the town of Brielle, these were probably Europe's first leading lights, though only intermittently lit during the fifteenth and sixteenth centuries.

The influence of the early monasteries has already been stressed: in the siting of churches at points useful to mariners, and in building stone towers on dangerous reefs, the monasteries on the Atlantic seaboard played a big part.

The first recorded man-made leading marks were two towers which, when seen in line, gave a safe entry into the harbour of Brielle at the mouth of the River Maas. Lights could be placed in the towers, which were financed by the herring fishery. In Scandinavia and North Germany, where sandy islands and dunes necessitated building timber structures, the first recorded kapen were erected, on the initiative and at the expense of the City of Lübeck, in 1410 on the southernmost tip of Skanör at Falsterbö (now in Sweden). At that time this was Danish territory and the Danish Kings were in perpetual conflict with the Hanse, of which Lübeck was then the acknowledged leader, but the importance of this passage apparently overcame whatever territorial and technical problems there were: the kapen were erected for the benefit of all sailors, but principally for those of the Hanse who were then at the height of their power and influence. In the Netherlands, the growing herring fishery caused the Zierikzee authorities to erect on the island of Schouwen two kapen which gave the fishermen a clear lead in from the North Sea. Later, in the fifteenth century, the city of Bremen was given permission by the territorial owner, the Hauptling of Jeverland, to erect kapen on the important mid-channel sandbank, the Mellumplatte, which stood in the approaches to the River Weser and the De Jaade roadstead. So low-lying is the coast at this point that a prominent recognition mark must have been essential for inward-bound shipping. In 1539 two timber kapen were erected by the city of Emden on the Dutch island of Rottum, placed so that when lined up they led to the entrance to the Wester Ems from which a line of seetonnen marked the deep-water channel. In 1567 a substantial tower was built on the island of Borkum to further help navigation in the outer Ems. This tower was 41m high and so constructed that when the mariner was entering or leaving the River Ems on the correct bearing he could see through the slit windows. Later in the sixteenth century two further kapen were erected on the small island of Bant which was closer to the coast than Borkum. These indicated the channel of the Ooster-Ems, which was useful for vessels approaching from or leaving for the east. Later again, in 1635, a kape was erected on Borkum so that, in line with the tall tower on Borkum, it indicated the Hubertplatte, a dangerous bank in the fairway of the Wester Ems. (See also Chapter III.)

Somewhat different was the Ros-bake, a very tall and prominent recognition mark on the edge of the Elbe main channel at Cuxhaven. This wooden structure, erected first in 1470 by the city of Hamburg and frequently rebuilt after storms, was 130ft high in 1743 and by far the biggest and most ambitious kape at that time in the world. It gave a high, clear indication of the true mouth of the Elbe and was replaced by a lighthouse in 1801. The Hamburg authorities by this time had also erected a kape near the Neuwerk tower, on a bearing that indicated the dangerous Scharhoorn reef.

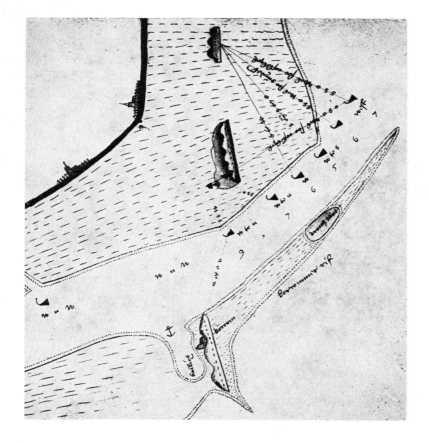

A very early chart of 1565 showing the Western Ems with buoyed channel and two kapen (leading marks) on the island of Rottum which give a transit line leading to the outermost buoy. (A. W. Lang, Geschichte des Seezeichenwesens)

Farther out in the North Sea approaches to the Elbe, the Hamburghers encountered a lot of difficulty with the inhabitants of Helgoland, who had made a good living from the wreck goods which so often found their way to the shores of this isolated community. However, in 1532 two timber kapen were built to mark some dangerous submerged rocks south of the harbour. These were replaced by more substantial kapen in 1633.

Meanwhile, between 1597 and 1601, the Grafen von Oldenburg, anxious to provide clear leading marks for the outer approaches to the Weser, and no doubt at the prompting of the Bremen authorities, built a tall stone tower on the island of Wangerooge. It had a lofty central spire which was easy to recognize from seaward, and two smaller spires so oriented that when kept in line with each other they led on a safe bearing to the first sea-tonne of the outer Weser.

In England the first lit leading marks were built during the reign of Henry VIII at the mouth of the River Tyne, which was beginning to be important for coal exports. By 1492 the Guild of Holy Trinity of Newcastle already existed as a charitable and religious institution with a predominantly maritime membership, for in that year it purchased the site of the present day Trinity House of Newcastle. In 1536 the Guild obtained a charter from Henry VIII to 'build and embattle' two towers, one at the entrance to the Haven of Tyne and the other on the hill adjoining. Conveniently, the Black Friars monastery was surrendered and dissolved three years later in 1539, so the stones from the monastery could be used to build the towers. Work began at the North Shields site in 1540. The lower tower was built on the eastward (or seaward) side of the Pow Burn, just where it flowed into the Tyne at the Narrows, only 120 yards wide. The high tower was built at the top of a steep bank west of the Pow Burn. The original charter stipulated that a light was to be maintained in each tower every night, for the support of which the Guild was authorized to receive 4d from every foreign ship and 2d from every English ship arriving at the port. The towers must have been quickly completed, for the Trinity accounts mention various payments in 1540 for 'the carrying of stones', blocks and pulleys, the hire of a boat, and finally in 1540 a sum was paid to a Mr Redhede 'for dawbing the two hawses at Shells'.

The keeper of the lights was at first a Will Davy, who was paid 20 shillings a year to keep a single tallow candle burning in each tower from three-eighths flood to half ebb at night. Candles were considered expensive: the Guild bought a dozen pounds of candles from a woman in 1541 for 18 pence, so the time and tide limit in the burning of candles was both sensible and economic. The main purpose of the towers and the lights was to guide vessels past the stony Tynemouth Barres, a shoal bank stretching from the north side across the river entrance. Since the bank shifted from time to time, it is not surprising to find that the alignment of the lights had sometimes to be changed. In 1542, only two years after the towers had been built, a sum of 12 pence was paid to Robert Stamper for spending two days in 'paralling the hawses'. The Great Rutter in common use in the seventeenth century, in describing the entry to the Tyne, warned: 'Take heed of your beacons, which is two little white houses, and one standeth upon the cliff and the other standeth upon the sands beneath, and also bring them together one above the other – and if he be just beside it by night there is in one of them a light.' In 1658 the towers were actually rebuilt in timber to facilitate their frequent realignment.

The accounts of the Newcastle Trinity House show a steady increase in authorized tolls from the original 2d to 6d for English ships, and from 4d to 1s 4d for foreign ships by 1613. They also show frequent small expenditures for mending broken windows after storms. One and later two candles were burnt in each tower, but there is no mention of the use of reflectors. Since burnished dishes were often used elsewhere as reflectors, it seems unlikely that the canny Tynesiders failed to adopt such a device. Copper and steel reflectors were certainly being installed elsewhere in the eighteenth century.

A sixteenth century map of the Chase of Rising, just to the north of King's Lynn, shows two timber kapen built on a hill between Wolverton and Sandringham (see Chapter IV). They appear to be aligned to lead into the inner channel to Lynn, and the map maker suggests that they may have been provided with fire baskets because they had ladders incorporated in their timbers. They were certainly not typical lever lights (described in Chapter VII).

Part of Greenvile Collins' chart of the mouth of the River Tyne showing the two lit leading marks on the north shore which give a safe course over the bar. Note also the landfall fire tower within the precincts of Tynemouth Castle. Drawn about 1690. Each of Collins' charts was dedicated to a different influential person or body.

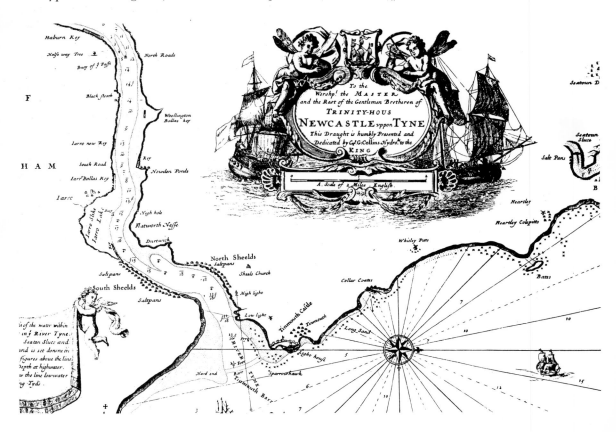

In 1674 three Brethren of the Newcastle Trinity House set out for the Humber to advise the authorities there on the erection of leading marks on Spurn Point; evidently Newcastle had achieved a reputation as pioneers, and it seems highly probable from this bit of evidence that the two Tynemouth towers were the first two leading marks, or at any rate the first leading lights, to be built in England. The Spurn leading marks were a pair of coal burning 'swape' or lever lights such as were often used in Denmark and in Dutch inshore waters.

The greatest pioneers in both the construction of leading marks and the building of fire towers (see Chapter VII) were the Dutch. The sixteenth century charts of L. J. Waghenaer and W. J. Blaeu clearly show that the Dutch employed timber kapen to mark the deepest channel from the North Sea into the sheltered roadstead of the Texel Stroom, the gateway to Amsterdam, Hoorn, Enkhuizen and other ports of the Zuider Sea, now known as the Ijselmeer. On the mainland side of the channel on the Spit of Huysduinen two kapen were aligned to show the deepest water in the Spaniard's Gat. Church towers on the south end of Texel were also used as lead marks for lesser and more difficult passages through the sandbanks. Farther south, the important sea-to-waterway passage south of the island of Goeree known as Brouwers Gat was indicated by two kapen on the land at the south of the island.

In western France the nature of the coast demanded the erection of stone beacon towers on key outlying rocks commanding the entrances of important harbours such as Brest, Cameret, Morlaix and Roscoff. At an early date local people began to place whitewashed pyramidal or cylindrical pillars on outlying rocks so that the line of transit between the foreground pillar and a prominent church steeple behind gave safe passage between the numerous reefs. Thus, on the Isle de Batz, which shelters the ancient drying harbour of Roscoff, a white pyramid was built on a rocky islet, in such a position that a sailor approaching from the east could, by keeping it in line with the spire of the church on the island, pass safely inshore of a rocky reef half a mile long. A cylindrical tower was built on a half-tide rock so that, kept in line with the church spire of Roscoff, a safe and deep channel could be followed to the entrance of the harbour. (This is illustrated in Chapter I.) In other localities chapels were specially built on the summits of rocky hills to serve as the back mark for a long and difficult channel, the front mark being either some natural above-water rock, or a tower built on a half-tide rock.

In England we have a good record of the state of leading marks, lights, fire towers and beacons at the end of the seventeenth century, for Captain Greenvile Collins had been appointed Hydrographer to King Charles II in 1682, with the specific charge of surveying the coasts and harbours of the British Isles. He spent seven years in doing this and finally reported to Charles' nephew, King William III. His charts and sailing directions were only published much later, in 1753 when they were well out of date, for they show neither the Eddystone Light nor England's first lightship at the Nore. They do, however, show Trinity

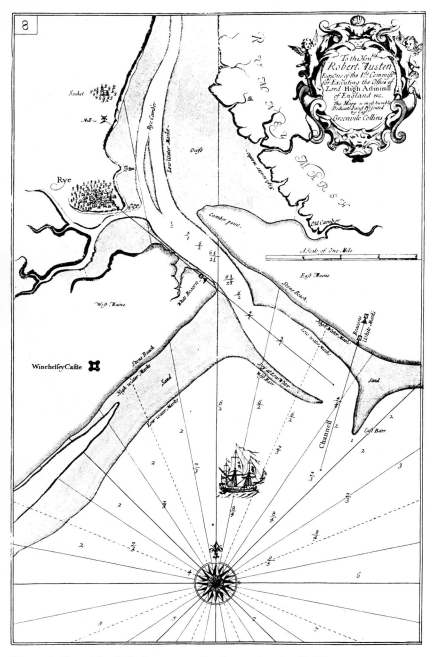

Part of Greenvile Collins' chart of Rye Harbour entrance showing two sets of leading marks placed to indicate a sharp change of course just within the bar.

House's first big lighthouse on St Agnes in the Scillies.

The most complex system of leading marks and lights at the end of the seventeenth century was that which gave safe entry and departure for Yarmouth Roads, then a centre of the North Sea herring industry and also an important haven of refuge for colliers and other cargo vessels plying between Tyne and Thames. At the northern entrance to the roads, two lighted towers on the high ground of Winterton Ness

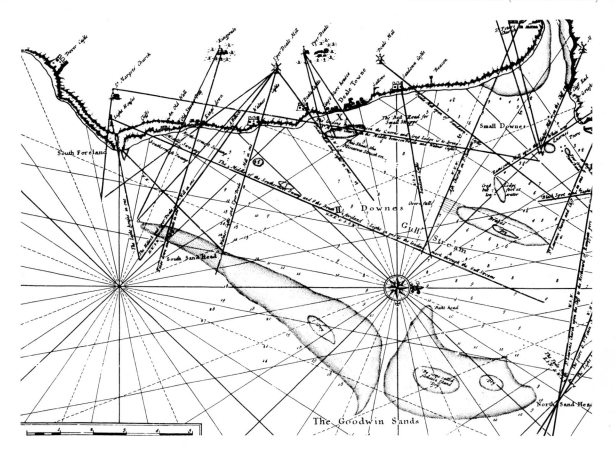

Part of Greenvile Collins' chart of the Kent Downs and South Foreland. Note the profusion of leading lines which use windmills, churches and natural cliff features, but the important transit south of the Goodwin Sands (left) is shown by the two lighthouses 'in one'.

gave a leading line on a SW–NE bearing which would bring ships safely close to the coast, where they picked up two more leading marks on a more southerly bearing which guided them inshore of the Middlefoote Sands. There were then two further leading marks with lights at Caister, which indicated a safe passage southeast for a southbound vessel, or reciprocally for a northbound vessel leaving the roads. The southern approach to the roads was indicated by two lit leading marks at Lowestoft, which took the ship inshore of the Corton and Home Sand. (See also Chapter VIII.)

Farther south, two leading marks, lit as fire towers at night, on Orford Ness gave a safe line between the Shipwash Sands and the Aldeburgh Knaps. Harwich was much used and had two light towers which, when placed in line, indicated the final approach to the port from the southeast. Still farther south, in the Thames approaches, the dangerously shallow Spitts passage from the Wallet into the main King's Channel and Swin was marked only by a buoy and by land features such as The Naze headland and church spires and towers near Clacton.

Specially built leading marks for entering river estuaries were located at Taymouth near Dundee, at Blythe in Northumberland, at

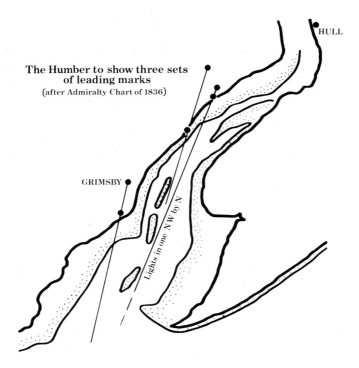

HULL

The Humber to show three sets
of leading marks
(after Admiralty Chart of 1836)

GRIMSBY

Lights in one NW by N

*River Humber leading marks
in the nineteenth century.
(Drawn by A. Peacock from
a contemporary Admiralty
chart)*

Tynemouth at the entrance to the River Deben near Felixstowe, and at
Rye. Some of these were of stone and had fires or lights, but others were
timber tripods similar to the Dutch and German kapen. At Spurn
Point on the Humber the two lit leading marks were placed to give a
safe easterly bearing south of the Dreadful Shoal. It is interesting to
note from Greenvile Collins' charts that, apart from the tripod beacon
at Black Rock, the only leading line for the port of Liverpool at the end
of the seventeenth century was Bootle windmill in line with a clump of
trees on a hillside farther east. For entrance to Portsmouth and
Spithead a natural leading line between Gilkicker Point and Stoke
Church was used. The first recorded leading or range marks in
America were two light towers placed in line on Plumb Island to show
the safe channel to Newburyport, on the Merrimack River whose
entrance has a bar and shoals. They were built in 1786.

In the last three hundred years the development of leading marks
has been considerable, but it is very much linked with the development
of lighthouses. In the Humber, a difficult tidal river with constantly
shifting shoals, two leading lights were built at Killingsholme in 1836 to
direct ships up the main channel from south of Spurn Point, and a few
years later additional leading lights were built at Killingsholme, Paull
and Thorngumbald to guide ships up the winding channel to Hull.
The low lights of the latter were on rails so that they could be realigned
when the deep-water channels shifted.

Smaller harbours continue to use unlit stone, timber or metal lattice
leading marks, but in rocky areas with narrow channels the tendency

has been to build leading marks taller so that the back one stands out from the visual 'clutter' of the background. Tall steel lattices painted in black and white horizontal bands with luminous paint patches tend to show up well from a distance. The front mark is always shorter and carries a distinctive symbol, such as a triangle or ball, so that it may be easily recognized. Mixed occulting and fixed lights, sometimes green or red, were useful for leading lights until recently, but the growth of ferry traffic using harbours with very little searoom has led to development of leading lights emitting powerful isophase (equal interval between light and dark) flashes from xenon discharge chambers which can be seen as easily by day as by night.

Diagram to show the modus operandi of a single-station direction light. Equipped with intense light sources, this can replace twin leading marks or lights. The transition between adjacent colours is very sharp, and the boundary can be used as a bearing or position line.

A single direction light projector which can show one or more colours. (AB Pharos Marine Ltd)

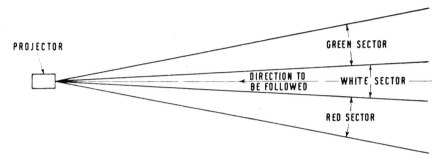

PROJECTOR

GREEN SECTOR

DIRECTION TO BE FOLLOWED — WHITE SECTOR

RED SECTOR

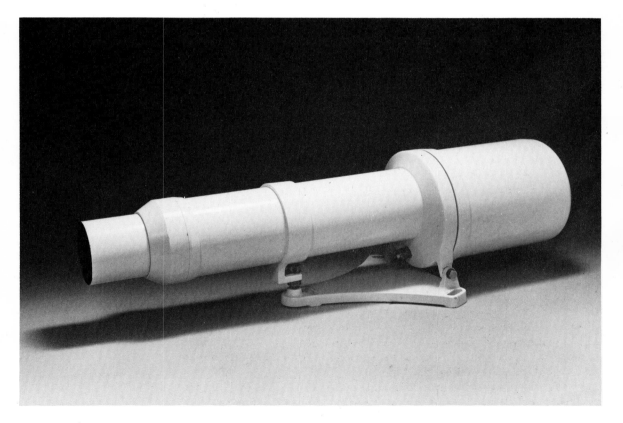

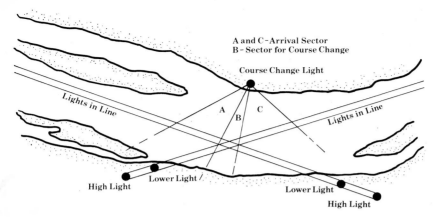

A and C - Arrival Sector
B - Sector for Course Change

Course Change Light

Lights in Line

A
B
C

Lights in Line

High Light

Lower Light

Lower Light

High Light

A modern leading light system for an estuary channel.

In navigable rivers with many bends, the leading mark principle is still extensively used so as to enable the pilot to keep in the centre of the channel. Each pair of leading marks has a symbol or letter as topmark, to avoid confusing part of one pair with another. The modern alternative to pairs of leading lights is a high-powered sector light bright enough to be seen by day and by night. It is powered by a 250W tungsten halogen lamp. A narrow central white sector is flanked by sharply defined green and red beams. The transition between sectors is less than a metre wide per nautical mile distance off. The beam angle can be varied between 5° and 20° to suit the local need.

Sources for Chapter VI

A. Ashley
W. J. Blaeu
G. Collins
Crommelin and van Suchtelen
M. M. Dodds
A. W. Lang
N. Long
M. A. Lower
A. Storey, (1) and (2)

VII
Fire Towers and Primitive Lights

Since man first learned to control fire he has probably used it for signalling. As every youthful student of the Wild West knows, the American Plains Indians were expert at sending coded puffs of smoke into the upper air. Europeans, handicapped by strong winds and low cloud, also used hilltop fires as a way of passing messages over great distances, and there is every reason to believe that when man began to trade by sea and send out fishing boats he used clifftop fires both as guiding lights for returning convoys and as warnings of enemy approach. The tower built on the island of Pharos was a model for a more sophisticated method of helping sailors to make a landfall. The Romans copied the idea, and in conformity with the character of their state the Roman Pharos became as much a military signal station as a navigational aid. The heirs of Roman civilization in France adopted the same attitude; their important strategic fire towers were called *phare*, though they used a different word, *fanal*, for the simple guiding lantern of a harbour.

The problem with all man-made fire structures was not so much the expense of building as the difficulties of manning, the organization of fuel collection and the maintenance of a good fire in all winds and weathers. For a period in Roman history the solution was found in a militaristic and totalitarian society which had an ample reserve of slave labour, but as the Empire declined the warring peoples of Europe lacked the organization to keep existing towers in repair and manned. There is historical and traditional evidence, however, that fires have been lit in times of war or during the passage of convoys. The concentration of Mediterranean seapower during the later Crusades provided a strong stimulus both to the building of new fire towers and to the repair and re-establishment of ancient structures.

As the power of Venice increased in the Adriatic and Mediterranean, seaborne trade, often in convoy, called for an organization to light the guiding fires for the fleets. Similarly, as sailing ship design improved in northern Europe and as both the herring industry and the power of the Hanseatic League grew, the volume of trade increased dramatically so that, for mutual protection, ships

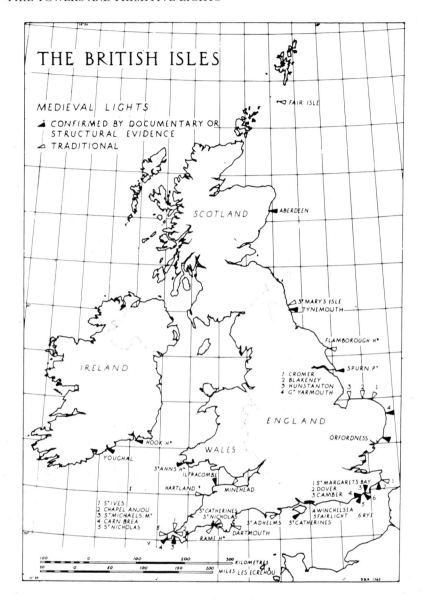

moved in convoy at the more favourable times of year. The lighting of fires on hills and towers might have been directed by orders conveyed in advance by fast sailing boats travelling ahead of the main convoy, and then by fast horsemen.

During the period 800 to 1200 AD the rebuilding and recommissioning of fire towers was counterbalanced by their sacking and destruction by warring factions. Thus, though it is probably true that a new fortified fire tower was erected on the island of Corduan at the mouth of the River Garonne by Louis the Pious, son of Charlemagne, and that Charlemagne repaired the Tour d'Ordre at Boulogne, many exposed beacons and hermits' chapels must have been

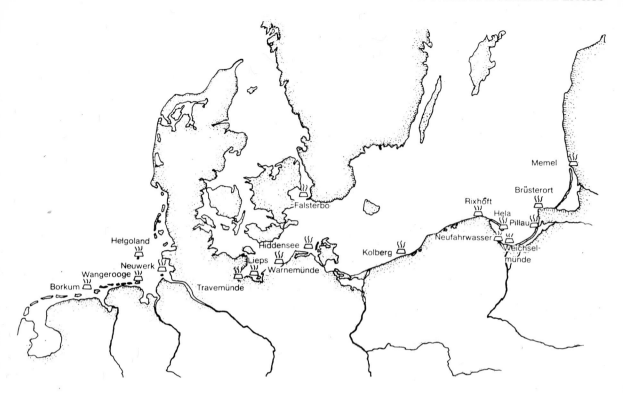

The sites of early German fire towers in the lower Baltic and North Sea: Falsterbo 1222, Travemünde 1226, Lieps, Wismar 1266, Hiddensee 1306, Warnemünde 1348, Weichselmünde 1482, Hela 1482, Pillau 1526. (F-K. Zemke)

destroyed in Viking raids. In the Mediterranean, the wars resulting from the rivalry between the merchants of Genoa and Pisa, and between the Guelphs and Ghibellines, resulted in the destruction of the isolated sea-girt tower on the rocky shoal of Meloria about 15 miles west of the River Arno and Pisa, and the building of new fortified light towers near the ports of the victorious faction. Venice, which was steadily increasing its power and influence, had some sort of light tower before 1000 and two further lights were established in the fourteenth century at the entrance to the lagoon.

In the Baltic, about 1220 a fire beacon was built on the top of a rounded hill on the headland of Falsterbo, the southern-most point of modern Sweden. It was probably an open brazier fire, for the hill is still known as Kolabacken or Coal Hill.

From the twelfth century onwards in North Europe the wealth and power of the Catholic Church was increasing, and it is not surprising to find that the humanitarian activities of coastal hermitages, convents and monasteries began to grow under the influence of that centralized power and the very real financial advantages accruing to coast watchers. The salvage of wreck goods and its resale back to the owners of the cargo could be followed by agreements between the local merchant mariners and the ecclesiastical authorities that tolls should be paid in return for the showing of a light at certain seasons.

The way in which these local arrangements developed is well illustrated by the story of the establishment of the first St Catherine's light, on the southern point of the Isle of Wight in England. In 1314 a cargo of wine owned by a monastery in Picardy was lost from a ship which foundered on the point. Much of the wine found its way into the hands of the local inhabitants, with or without the connivance of the crew. Protracted lawsuits culminated in an appeal to Rome which resulted in a local leader, Walter de Godeton, being forced under threat of excommunication to build an oratory and light tower dedicated to St Catherine. This was done by 1328 and the building lasted long enough for it to be properly surveyed and described in later years.

An even earlier ecclesiastical light was built in the late twelfth century by Fitzgerald on Hook Head, commanding the entrance to Waterford Harbour on the southern coast of Ireland, and it is recorded that in 1245 the Augustinian monks occupying the site had been given

St Catherine's Tower on Chale Down, Isle of Wight. Built in the fourteenth century as a seamark, but any light shown at this altitude must have been so dim as to be almost useless for mariners. (D. B. Hague)

the right to collect tolls from passing ships. A similar arrangement gave the responsibility of providing light, and the right to collect tolls, to the nuns of St Anne's convent farther south at Youghal. Irish towers of this period were probably similar to the low cottage-like buildings at Howth, Kinsale, Loop Head and Cross Isle which have been surveyed by the archaeologist D. B. Hague. He suggests that they burnt peat or coal.

By the fourteenth century there was a chapel on Rame Head commanding Plymouth Sound, and in the fifteenth century it is recorded that a watchman was being paid to keep alight a warning beacon fire. Similar fees were paid to Richard, the hermit of St Michael of Brae, near Land's End. The Black Prince, who had rebuilt and refortified the tower of Corduan on the Garonne, allowed the hermits living there to collect the tolls from the wine trade. There is good archaeological evidence of a stone cresset light kept by the monks on the top of the tower of the church on St Michael's Mount off the Channel coast of Cornwall. (A cresset is a vessel filled with oil or grease containing a floating wick.)

A coal fire was maintained on a tower of the priory built on Tynemouth Cliff before this was replaced by Tynemouth Castle in Tudor times: it was apparently unreliable, for sixteenth century seafarers complained that fires were not lit and tolls too high. There is also evidence of a light from St Ninian's Chapel on Castle Hill, Aberdeen. A hermit's chapel dedicated to St Edmund and built on Hunstanton Cliffs in northwest Norfolk may have shown a light to guide ships into the Wash and Lynn, though there is no record of tolls being paid. The same applied to the hermitage of St Margaret's Strait which stood on an important geographical site near the later position of the South Foreland lights.

Seamarking in the lower Baltic was relatively well advanced in Medieval times, due to the importance of the Baltic herring fishery and the influence of the early Hanseatic traders. It is certain that some form of light was displayed at seven sites before 1500, including Falsterbo, already mentioned, Travemunde (entrance to Lübeck), Warnemunde (entrance to Rostock) and Weichselmunde (entrance to Danzig).

A disproportionate drawing of a gibbet-lantern hanging from a fire tower. From a chart of 1572, it may represent the light of Warnemünde. (A. W. Lang, Geschichte des Seezeichenwesens*)*

Lights were only shown at certain times, when the fishing fleet was out or a trading convoy was expected. Single candles were used within lanterns after glass became available in the thirteenth century, but coal in braziers was used for the more important sites as a single candle viewed through smoky glass was too feeble to be seen from any distance. Coal braziers on whipstaffs, known in German as *Steinkohlenwippe* (and in English as swapes or poppinjays) were often used.

An important piece of historical evidence from the Humber region gives us a clue as to the possible relationship between the Trinity Guilds of merchant mariners, the local port authorities and the hermits who chose to lead their solitary and contemplative lives in remote places. In 1369 the Trinity Guild of Hull was founded; half a century later the port had enough political influence for King Henry VI to grant the Mayor the right to collect dues from every ship entering the Humber. The dues were for completion, maintenance and lighting of a tower being built by Richard Reedbarrow, the hermit of the Chapel of St Mary and St Anne, to serve as a beacon by day and a light by night on Spurn Point. This tower may have been engulfed by the sea, for a description of Edward IV's landing there in 1471 makes no mention of it, and in 1674 the Hull authorities were asking for the assistance of Trinity House of Newcastle in building two leading lights on the point.

Secular authorities also controlled some seamarks and fire towers in medieval England, notably around Rye and Winchelsea on the South Coast where the tolls went to the Barons of the Cinque Ports. At Great Yarmouth, where the growth of the herring industry and the relatively safe anchorage of Yarmouth had caused great concentrations of shipping and the buildup of strong financial interests, another light was built. The story of these conflicting financial interests and the fight for lighthouse provision and tolls belongs in Chapter VIII.

The problem of piracy, which in England had been only partly controlled by the strong naval policy of the Plantagenets, was the main obstacle to the provision of navigational aids elsewhere in North Europe. Danish pirates and marauders were the scourge of the early Baltic traders, but the Peace of Stralsund in 1350 gave a respite.

We have to turn to Flanders to learn more of the technical developments. At Brielle, a small town south of the Maas Sluis and now close to Rotterdam, and at Nieuwpoort at the mouth of the River Yser, there were already fire towers in the thirteenth century. By 1366 there were similar installations at Dunkirk, Ostende and Blankenberg, and in 1370 one was built at West Kapelle on the island of Walcheren. These towers were thus grouped around the estuaries of the West and East Schelde, and no doubt reflected the growing wealth and importance of Flanders' textile and ceramic industries, as well as the difficulty and complexity of its waterways. By the end of the fifteenth century more towers had been built at Heyst in Flanders and at Goeree, Huysduinen, Texel, Vlieland and Terschelling farther north. Some of these were small huts or *vuurboeten*, built, maintained and lit as required by local fishermen.

Technical information is scanty, but the tall tower at Brielle known as the Steenebake was constructed around a wooden framework and topped by a small oak-framed glasshouse in which candles were burnt. The other early tower at Nieuwpoort was built of brick and had a partly enclosed brick hearth at its summit; here bundles of dried reeds provided the light. At Ostende there is a record of oil lamps being used, but experiments with oil burning were usually unsuccessful in the Middle Ages either because of expense or the danger of fire. All the old fire towers had to have sheds for fuel and skilled men to maintain the fires. It seems that there was at this time no really satisfactory light source and various towers at various times burnt peat, straw, birchwood blocks and oak. Bellows of the type used in forges were

The Nieuwpoort fire tower which burned reed bundles as a light source from the fourteenth century onwards. A 1822 lithograph of the ruin. (A. W. Lang, Geschichte des Seezeichenwesens*)*

usually needed, but the light from such fires was rarely visible for more than about 7 sea miles.

From the end of the sixteenth century through the eighteenth there was an increasing trend towards the use of open coal fires, using the best seacoal imported from Newcastle and Northern Britain. Such fires, if properly controlled, could often be seen for more than 7 miles, particularly if the glow was reflected by the undersides of low clouds. Dutch light-keepers had by this time gained considerable experience in

Fire tower at Petten, North Netherlands in 1605. Wood or reed bundles were used as fuel. (A. W. Lang, Geschichte des Seezeichenwesens)

designing fire towers of stone, brick and wood, with the necessary skills in maintaining good safe fires. Open coal fires were known to the Dutch and Germans as *Bluse* and the skilled man who kept them as a *Blusenmeister*. The name derives from an old Low German word for blower or bellows, and clearly bears a similarity to the English word 'blaze'.

Steinkohlbluse towers were usually square with 3–4km wide sides and a height of about 12m. The upper hearth floor was often roofed by a spire through which passed a central chimney. The sides of the upper hearth floor were protected by small leaded windows. To protect the windows from too much heat the fire was contained in a clay stove aerated by fixed bellows. There were usually two blusenmeisters at work at any one time; accidents due to storm damage and out-of-control fires were a constant threat. Towers at remote sites tended to have open hearths, but those near other dwellings had enclosed grates the fire in which was controlled by bellows, often operated by a blacksmith.

On the Frisian island of Terschelling an experiment with an iron basket full of burning coals, held clear of the tower by a chain run through a gantry or gibbet, was a variation of the Kohlenwippe principle of raising a burning brazier to a height. These fire-levers were known as swapes in England, as Wypfeuer or Kohlenwipper in Germany and as poppinjays in Denmark. The word 'poppinjay' derives from *pappagei* or parrot, a wooden representation of which was often used as a jousting target. Presumably the fire levers looked sufficiently like the wooden target to earn their extraordinary

A swape or lever light, also known as a poppinjay. Coal was used as fuel in the mobile brazier. (D. B. Hague)

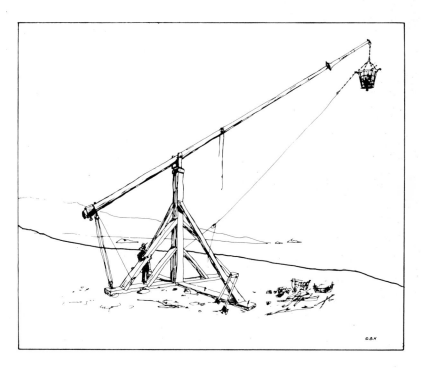

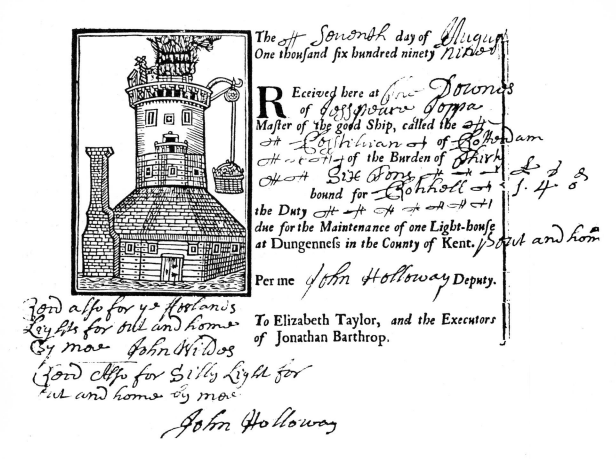

Receipt for Light Dues for Dungeness Light in 1699. Note the open fire, the crane for hoisting fuel and the fuelstore. The certificate is recorded as good for the Scilly and Foreland lights as well as Dungeness. (A. W. Lang, Geschichte des Seezeichenwesens)

nickname. They were used in the Netherlands, in the Baltic and at some English East Coast estuaries, e.g. Spurn Point.

In England coal fire lights were established at the North and South Forelands in 1636. They were built of wood, but after a fire the North Foreland was rebuilt in flint and brick. Trinity House of Deptford built a coal-fired light on St Agnes, the southernmost of the Isles of Scilly, before the end of the seventeenth century, while an important wooden fire tower with fuel stores, living accommodation and a crane for hoisting fuel to the lantern was erected by a private patentee on Dungeness west of Dover. Tolls were charged for vessels passing the Point and collected in the Custom Houses. Towers, whether regularly lit or not is uncertain, had been built on Rame Head south of Plymouth, at Flamborough Head, on the Farne Islands and at the Old Head of Kinsale in Southern Ireland. Leading lights using glass protected candles had been built, as already described, earlier in the sixteenth century in the Tyne, and by the end of the seventeenth century there were ten pairs of leading lights on the East Coast of England and a further pair at the entrance to the Tay near Dundee. Headland fire towers are shown by Greenvile Collins on St Anne's Head, Milford Haven, the North Foreland, Flatholme in the Bristol

Channel and the Isle of May in the Firth of Forth. A tower at Foulness Point in Norfolk had been built but not yet lit.

Dutch fire-keepers and designers such as Cornelious Vinck and later Berends tried to sell their expertise to the King of Denmark and the North German cities. Fire towers were built near Copenhagen between 1560 and 1588, and later at Skagen on the northernmost point of Denmark and on the island of Anholt in the Kattegat. In 1563 a fire tower was erected on the headland of Kullen (now in Sweden). In 1629 light towers were built at Falsterbo and on the islands of Laeso and Nidingen in the Kattegat. The Danes found that burning tar and pitch was unsatisfactory and at Skagen they experimented with a kohlenwippe. This too was unsatisfactory, so they switched to burning fish oil and later, in 1623, to coal. In the end most towers switched to coal as the supplies from England became more plentiful and cheaper; it was by far the most reliable light source at the time, and presumably candle lanterns had proved too feeble for landfall marks on the Continental coast of the North Sea. It has been suggested that the coldness of the winter in those areas prevented the vaporisation of oil and that coal was both more efficient and more comfortable than candles.

By 1630 there was a coal light on Helgoland, a year later one on Wangerooge and in 1644 one in the Neuwerk tower. Borkum did not get a light until 1780.

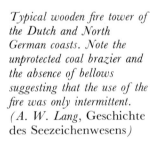

Typical wooden fire tower of the Dutch and North German coasts. Note the unprotected coal brazier and the absence of bellows suggesting that the use of the fire was only intermittent. (A. W. Lang, Geschichte des Seezeichenwesens)

The story of early fire towers in France is in many ways different from the rest of Europe. Prior to the beginning of the seventeenth century there were a number of fanals or lanterns to be found on the battlements of defensive towers on various sites on the Mediterranean coast, notably Aigues Mortes and the Ilot du Planier outside Marseilles Harbour, on the clock tower of Dunkerque church, in the Tour de Garrot at La Rochelle, and possibly at St Mathieu Monastery near Ushant. These were regarded as signals to warn of pirate raids rather than navigational aids, but as the seventeenth century progressed glass lanterns were made and fish oil burners provided the light. We also read more of the requests of seafarers for navigational aids. The Tour de Corduan in the approaches to Bordeaux, which was built, rebuilt and embellished from 1590 through to 1660 during the reigns of several kings, was when completed a noble feat of architecture. As a navigational beacon it was unnecessarily elaborate and the inhabitants of Aquitaine objected to the imposts which successive kings demanded from them in order to complete the tower. It housed a small garrison as well as showing an oil light. Nearby to the north, the busy port of La Rochelle and the city of Rochefort on the River Charente attracted a

Ancient and Modern. Modern lighthouse and Coastguard station built among the ruins of the Monastery of St Mathieu near Brest. The monks provided an early pilotage and salvage service and possibly provided a light. The short tower (left) is the site of the old light built at the end of the eighteenth century; it now serves as a Coastguard and signal station. (Photo Martin Collins)

great deal of sea trade, and the Minister of Marine, Colbert, received many requests to have lights placed at the northwestern extremities of the islands of Ré and Oléron because many ships were cast away on these rocky points each year. In response to these requests the light tower of Chassiron was erected on Oléron and Les Baleines on Ré. Although Vauban was at the end of the seventeenth century busy building *tours bastionées* all around the coasts of France, he made more provision for naval signalling than for navigational aids in his fortresses. The three towers of Corduan, Chassiron and Baleines were the only ones specifically built for navigators. There was a surge of activity at the end of the century when it was realized how far behind England France had fallen in the provision of lights. Indeed, we find in 1700 Mr St Lo, Marine Superintendent at Plymouth, writing to M. de Combes, his opposite number in Normandy, requesting a light at Barfleur, two on Ushant and several in other places dangerous to ships of all nations. By 1699 the Phare du Stiff on Ushant had been built, St Mathieu had a regular lighthouse and keeper, Cap Fréhel near St Malo and Calais had been lighted, while there were two coal-fired towers on Cap de la Heve at the entrance to Le Havre and the Seine.

The early fire towers cannot really be classed as lighthouses. The French distinguished between a 'fanal' or minor light and a 'phare'; the latter were not established until the eighteenth century in France. The function of many fire towers was to cast a glow into the sky which would be visible by night and a big plume of smoke visible by day, to facilitate landfalls and a measure of coastal recognition. Early experiments using fish oil burners with linen wicks were not successful outside France and the use of fuels other than sea coal from Britain was found to be expensive, laborious and inefficient. The dangers to the tower and its guardian were considerable. It is not certain why the English favoured glass-protected candles as a light source when they had a cheap source of coal on their doorstep, but the probable answer is that the English used coal fires for headland and landfall towers such as those at St Agnes, Dungeness and Kinsale, while they stuck to the more predictable but expensive candles for lights close to habitation.

Sources for Chapter VII

G. Collins
Cromellin and van Suchtelen
M. M. Dodds
R. Faille
D. B. Hague
D. B. Hague and R. Christie
H. Henningsen
A. W Lang
A. Storey, (i)
F-K. Zemke

VIII
Profit and Philanthropy 1600–1800

The story of the growth of seamarking in the seventeenth and eighteenth centuries, which has been already touched on, is one which both reflects and illuminates the accelerating growth of sea trade. The social and financial changes which followed trade expansion were every bit as cataclysmic as the consequences of the introduction of microchip electronics in our own times. Then as now, there was an alteration in the relative wealth of both geographical areas and social groups. The money invested in and reaped from ship-building, port improvements, warehousing and merchant activities in the seventeenth century was doubled and re-doubled, making thousands rich and powerful, some bankrupt, and many poor sailors dead by

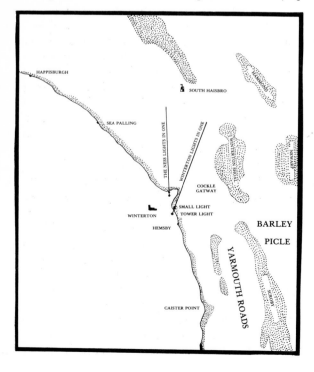

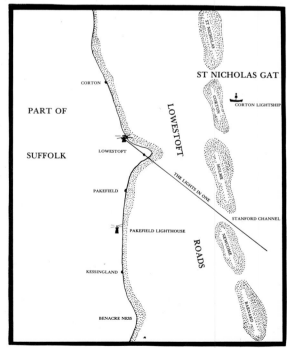

drowning. Everything connected with the sea, whether it was a transatlantic privateering venture, the building of a wharf, or the making of ropes and sails was full of risk and high profit. The diaries of Samuel Pepys give us an insight into the wealth of the Baltic traders and the money they were prepared to lay out in handsome gifts to smooth the way towards Navy contracts.

It was not only the opening of the Atlantic and Indian Oceans to European merchants but also the requirements of internal commerce which helped to power this enormous expansion of sea trade. The roads were rudimentary, and even by the beginning of the eighteenth century when Daniel Defoe made his fact-finding journeys through England they were still atrocious, especially in winter. Coal mining in Durham, Northumberland and Fife was not only bringing wealth to these areas but changing the habits of people in the South. The ships which carried coal from Newcastle to London, Hull, Lynn and Ipswich returned with cargoes of corn, cloth and other manufactured goods: there was no other way in which heavy loads could be carried. When Defoe recorded the state of England in 1727, the 'navigations' of the Ouse and other great rivers falling into the Humber were making the manufactures of such inland centres as Leeds, Bradford and Nottingham accessible to the sea by ship or barge. Furthermore, Great Yarmouth was beginning to rival the Dutch harbours as a centre for the herring trade.

The peculiarities of the East Anglian salient made the East Coast sea passage a nightmare for the small colliers and hoys. Sandbanks in a series of ridges running NE–SW near the outer Thames, more N–S off Norfolk and E–W towards the Wash offered the shipmaster a number of options, the safest of which, in the collective opinion of those times, was to hug the coast south of Winterton Ness at the northeast extremity of Norfolk. This choice was the more desirable because Yarmouth Roads, protected from the full force of the northeasterly winds by extensive outlying banks, offered safe anchorage in all winds from southwest through west to north. It is not surprising, therefore, that navigational aids were provided there from an early date. A light on Lowestoft Ness – the most easterly point of England – had been maintained intermittently from medieval times, and the Trinity House of Deptford was itself responsible for setting up two pairs of leading lights – the first at Caister in 1600 and the second at Lowestoft in 1609. The front lights were of latticed timber enclosing candle lanterns. Farther north there were two sets of leading lights, privately owned at Winterton, and set up by Trinity House on Winterton Ness. There were protracted legal squabbles between John Meldrum and the man to whom he sold his rights, Sir Edward Turnour, on the one hand and the Corporation of Trinity House on the other. The story of John Meldrum, who was one of the great entrepreneurs of lighthouse ownership, illustrates the importance of being a friend of the King when petitioning for a grant to build a lighthouse. He had come to England with James I and made his reputation as a soldier at La Rochelle and in Ireland. He first purchased the concession of

Map of northern entrance (Cockle Gat) to Yarmouth Roads to show the leading lights on Winterton Ness and at Winterton. (Neville Long, Lights of East Anglia*)*

Map to show the alignment of Lowestoft lights to lead through the Stanford Channel. (Neville Long)

Winterton from another, and then successfully obtained in his own name the right to build lighthouses on the North and South Forelands and at Orfordness in 1635. There were huge capital gains when these concessions eventually passed out of his hands.

The whole sorry story of the Winterton lights, and it was a muddled, bitter and confusing story which lasted from 1616 to 1685, shows the Masters and Brethren of Trinity House in a very poor light. They were concerned mainly for their charter rights (with attendant annual fees) and doing as little as possible in laying out money. When they did send Brethren to Winterton in order to survey the coast and to answer local pleas for leading marks and lights, as happened in 1615, 1677 and 1683, their decision was usually a negative one which stressed the difficulties, the changing channels, the coastal erosion and the lack of proven need. While these procrastinations continued, the list of lost ships and lost lives off Winterton grew. At least capitalists like Meldrum, Gore and Turnour were prepared to venture money and to build, even if their ultimate motive was profit and capital gain.

The Brethren of Trinity House did, however, comprehend better than the absent patentees the peculiar difficulties caused by the

The Hunstanton Cliff Light viewed through the ruins of St Edmund's Chapel. The site is a crucial fixing point for a vessel seeking to enter Lynn Haven and it is probable that a 'chapel light' was shown intermittently in the Middle Ages. (Neville Long)

frequent shifting of channels after winter storms. Reading about these seventeenth century legal actions, one cannot help but be shocked by the apparent absence of concern for the lives of seamen: they lived in cold and squalor aboard ship, endured frightening sleepless nights within the sound of broken water and took great risks to bring their cargoes home to port. On one night of storm in 1770 some 40 ships and over 200 lives were lost off the Norfolk coast. The Brethren were, of course, recruited from the most successful shipmasters and merchants as well as from the astute and knowledgeable, but it does seem that their overwhelming motive in those years was to avoid expenditure and to consolidate the income of the Corporation.

One of their number, Sir William Batten, Surveyor of the Navy and a colleague, neighbour and oftimes enemy of Samuel Pepys, seems to have used his position as Master in 1663 to further schemes of his own. In the year of his Mastership he probably influenced the Court of Trinity House not to oppose a royal grant to John Knight, who had applied to build lights by St Edmund's Chapel on Hunstanton Cliffs; and in the following year, when no longer Master, he successfully petitioned privately for the right to erect leading lights for Harwich and to collect tolls from all coastal shipping which passed them, even though the lights eventually displayed were only visible to ships approaching within a few miles of Harwich. 'Nice work, Sir William', a modern diarist might have noted, but Pepys simply minuted that it was 'a gift of a fortune'. Batten entrusted the care of the very inefficient Harwich lights to his negro servant Mingo, who continued to look after them after Batten died a few years later. Ownership passed via Batten's widow and a married granddaughter to the Rebow family, who became great local magnates and retained possession of these profitable lights right into the nineteenth century.

Trinity House did, however, in the seventeenth century complete and man the much-needed light on St Agnes, one of the Isles of Scilly.

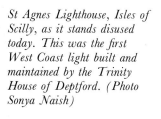

St Agnes Lighthouse, Isles of Scilly, as it stands disused today. This was the first West Coast light built and maintained by the Trinity House of Deptford. (Photo Sonya Naish)

It seems that at last they were gradually coming to terms with their true function as a public utility, ploughing back some of their profit from light dues and fees from private owners into buoyage and beaconage, especially in the Thames and its approaches.

In Scotland, where there was no chartered body to undertake responsibility for or to advise on the building of navigation aids, action usually had to wait on a prolonged process of petitioning, negotiation and consultation with the burghs and shipmasters by representatives of the King's Privy Council in Edinburgh. The coal-burning fire tower on the Island of May which commands the northeastern approaches to the Firth of Forth was first proposed eleven years before it was eventually built under letters patent granted to Maxwell, Cunningham and Geddes in 1636 by King Charles I. Tolls were to be levied by Customs officers in the ports of the Firth and there were penalties for letting a ship sail without first abstracting money from the captain, who was given a receipt. A penny per ton of goods was the going rate in England, but the first suggested toll for the May light of 2s Scots, which approximates to 2d English, was found to be more than the canny shipmasters were willing to pay. It seems from this Scottish evidence that a wide measure of agreement had to be reached with all the interested parties before the Crown would issue letters patent. 'No taxation without representation' was thus a principle accepted by the monarch; however, his own fee for the May patent was £1,000 (Scots) annually.

The Royal Burgh of Dundee had in 1606 obtained a charter from King James VI to take tolls from ships entering their harbour which was conditional on laying cask buoys to mark the difficult sand-girt channel of Taymouth, just south of Budden Ness. Probably these did not prove satisfactory, and even less satisfactory was the customary leading line of the Abbey in Arbroath in transit with a distant hill. Hence, in 1687 the Burgh of Dundee was granted the right to build on Dudden Ness two towers to be used as leading marks by day and be lit by coal fires by night. In return Dundee was empowered to levy

A receipt for Light Dues for passing the Isle of May. At the time, the coal-fired tower was Scotland's only landfall light. (Morton Muniments)

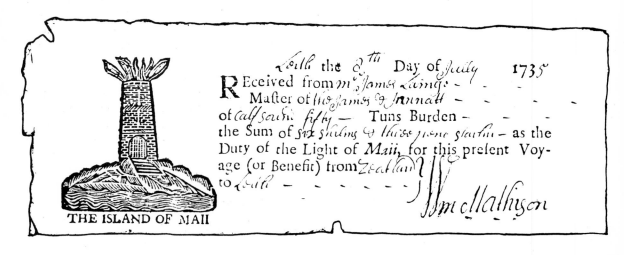

THE ISLAND OF MAII

appropriate tolls. Thus were built the first and, for very many years the only, leading lights in Scotland.

At an earlier time, Fife colliery owners and merchants had agreed to erect beacons and marks on the outlying rocks of the Firth at their own expense, but there is no evidence that they did so for none appear on Greenvile Collins' charts save the occasional pole beacon in the approaches to important harbours such as Leith and Aberdeen.

In Ireland and the Isle of Man there were a few pole beacons close to harbour entrances, e.g. Belfast. There were four fire towers, one on the Hill of Howth outside Dublin, one on the Old Head of Kinsale and one within the Kinsale Harbour entrance, and an old monastic light on Hook Head outside Waterford. Local authorities and fraternities of fishermen did their best to maintain the fires and beacons, but the Dublin port authorities were the only ones successful in collecting substantial tolls for the Howth light. Gradually Dublin took over the management of lights and beacons elsewhere in the country, until in 1786 an Act of the Irish Parliament set up a special Corporation to be officially responsible. This was the precursor of the Commission for Irish Lights, which was not set up until well into the nineteenth century.

In England one of the first of the new type of coal-fired lighthouses built on Dungeness had been in receipt of tolls since 1610 (which must have been immediately the light was lit), while the two towers built by John Meldrum on the South Foreland about 1620 gave a safe transit south of the Goodwin Sands. The inshore tower in line with a white patch on the cliffs near Walmer Castle gave a safe passage through the Gull Stream, inshore of the Goodwins, to the useful roadstead of the Downs. The North Foreland tower as rebuilt during the reign of James I was a substantial building which continued in service for over a hundred years. A light tower on the Lizard Point in Cornwall, built by the Cornish speculator, Killigrew, quickly went out of service because the owner could not collect the tolls to maintain it, nor gain the goodwill of the local population who had been used to making a better living from wrecks. The collection of tolls required a good measure of consent from shipmasters and merchants, but also considerable organization. Some of the big lighthouse owners used agents who employed subagents within the port Customs Houses. The full authority of the Customs House was useful in preventing ships from unloading or sailing before all tolls and dues had been collected.

The care and maintenance of these primitive lights posed problems, particularly in bad weather when protective glass was often shattered and smoke could obscure the light. A bad fire-keeper could waste coal and produce a bad light, but a skilled man deserved more than the £30 per annum he was paid. About 100 tons of coal was consumed in a year. Some keepers were neglectful of their duties and took part-time employment by day: one old gentleman at the Chapel Light at Hunstanton was said by a contemporary to have required a shot fired to wake him up and make him pump the bellows. Little progress was made in improving sources of illumination until towards the end of the eighteenth century, and coal despite its dangers and the labour of haulage was still preferred for isolated headland towers. Candle lanterns were used if the tower was near human habitation and in the front structures of leading lights. Coastal erosion caused many front structures on the East Coast to be washed away, and changing channels often required re-alignment of the front light, so they were usually constructed of timber so as to be more readily movable.

As the increase of trade, and of transatlantic shipping in particular, continued to accelerate, lighthouses came to be built in more difficult sites, but ones from which the ultimate profit would be considerable. The most famous example of capital venturing was Winstanley's tower on the Eddystone Rock 12 miles south of Plymouth: not only was this the first rock lighthouse to be built in North Europe (the twelfth century tower of Meloria built by the Pisans was the first in the world), but Winstanley was an ingenious and scientific man who was motivated more by the engineering challenge than by the hope of future profit from the English Channel shipping which was bound to pass his light and be liable to tolls. He did not live long enough to grow rich for he and his tower were swept away in the great storm of 1703. He had proved, however, that a candle-lit tower could be built on an isolated rock and that in five years there had been no loss of ships or lives. Thenceforward merchants and navigators would need no convincing of the value of rock lighthouses. The second Eddystone tower, built by Rudyerd and burned down 40 years later, illustrated the dangers inherent in keeping fires whether candle, oil or coal in these early structures.

The next rock light to appear was on the Skerries off Holyhead. Local shipmasters had been petitioning for a light since 1622, but Trinity House as usual made much of the difficulties and succeeded in blocking the proposed scheme until 1714 when John Trench succeeded in obtaining a patent. His coal-fired light cost £3000 to build and also took the life of his son and several labourers by drowning. When Trench himself died twelve years later it was thought that he had kept the fire at a loss and that certainly he had not recouped his capital. His heirs and assigns, however, were to be made rich by the Skerries for they were given the dues in perpetuity by Act of Parliament. One hundred years later the light was earning £12,500 annually after deducting all expenses, and in 1841, just after the Act of 1836 had vested all private lighthouses in Trinity House, a jury awarded the owners £444,984, surely one of the most remarkable capital gains on an original investment of £3,000.

The third Eddystone Light, designed by Smeaton to replace the burnt Rudyerd tower, was a masterpiece of careful mathematical calculation, shrewd engineering forethought, and a remarkable aesthetic yet practical appreciation that the completed tower should resemble the trunk of a mature English oak, broad at the base and tapering swiftly to its minimum load-bearing width. Its successful completion within three years, 1756–9, and its durability provided future designers with a proven basis for the wave-washed lighthouse of the future. Weston, the lessee of the patent, seems to have been a true philanthropist prepared to risk capital for the good of the seafaring community.

One more lighthouse was to be constructed on a site even more remote from the coast than the Eddystone, but the architect, a young man of twenty-four, was not influenced by Smeaton's design; or perhaps lack of capital was the reason for the adoption of an open-legged or trestle type of construction intended to allow the force of a wave to pass through the framework. The site chosen was the Smalls, a

The first Smalls Lighthouse. A drawing by D. B. Hague, based on a careful archeological survey of surviving post holes and an interpretation of contemporary descriptions.

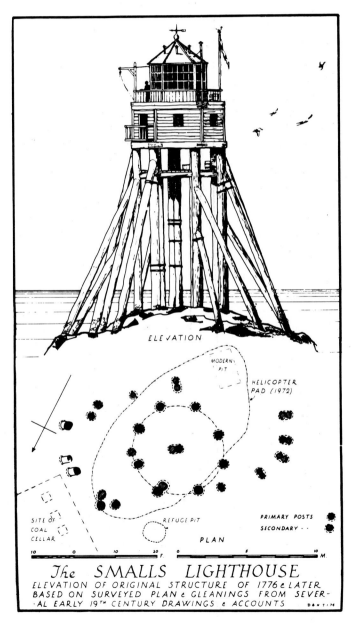

ELEVATION

MODERN PIT

HELICOPTER PAD (1972)

SITE OF COAL CELLAR

REFUGE PIT

PRIMARY POSTS

SECONDARY · ·

PLAN

The SMALLS LIGHTHOUSE
ELEVATION OF ORIGINAL STRUCTURE OF 1776 & LATER BASED ON SURVEYED PLAN & GLEANINGS FROM SEVER-AL EARLY 19TH CENTURY DRAWINGS & ACCOUNTS

99

low reef some 21 miles west of the Pembrokeshire coast at St David's, and the patentee, John Phillips, a local man who was the manager of Liverpool's northern dock, was well aware both of the importance of the light to ships making for Liverpool, Bristol and the Welsh ports and its future profitability. The building of this timber tower was a long and

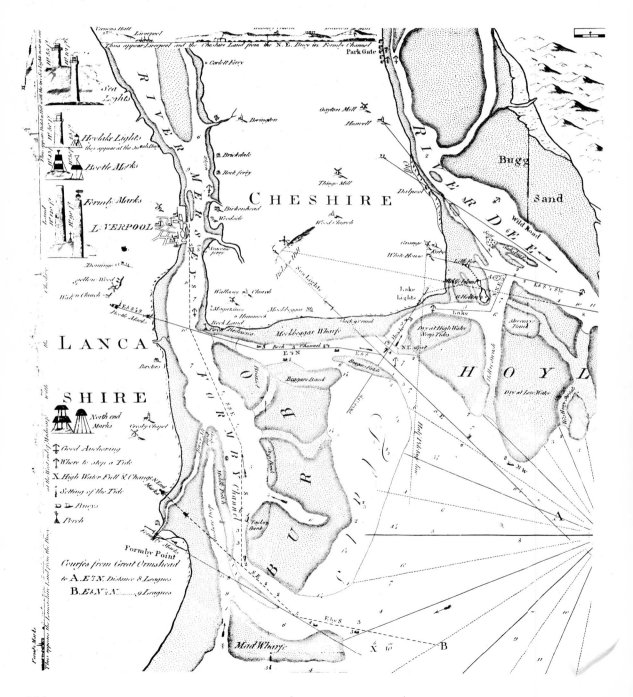

dangerous process (1774–6) and the necessity for frequent repairs to the structure in later years showed that there was really no substitute for the solid masonry tower. The keepers suffered untold hardships, battered by waves in their leaky cabin and frequently close to starvation when relief was delayed by storms. (The body of one keeper who was killed by an accident during a gale was preserved by a sole survivor for over two weeks until relief arrived, lest he should be suspected of murder. This event persuaded all lighthouse supervisors to insist thereafter on a complement of three for any rock station.) The Smalls proved in the end to be a great money spinner, however, for it was passed by nearly all transatlantic shipping out of West Coast ports as well as those in the coastal and Irish trade.

Foremost among the ports which in the eighteenth century tried to improve the safety of their entrances was Liverpool. It had supplanted Chester as the most important harbour in northwest England and began to develop its wharfage alongside the swift-flowing, deep River Mersey to accommodate the larger vessels of the American trade. The problem for Liverpool was its bar, on one side of which was the poorly protected roadstead of Hoylake. As we have seen, at the time of Greenvile Collins' survey, there was only one pole beacon at Black Rock on the northeastern tip of the Wirral Peninsula and two natural leading marks at Bootle to help the mariner into the anchorage. By 1710 the Formby Channel, which lay closest to the Lancashire coast and which had always been considered a minor one, was marked with two leading marks at Formby, two buoys and a shoreside perch beacon at Crosby.

Most ships for Liverpool, however, used Hoylake while waiting for a tide and thence when the tide served followed east along the Wirral coast inshore of the vast drying sand called the Burbo Flats. This was known as the Redd or Rock Channel, which joined the Mersey at the Black Rock Beacon. To help ships make their way into the Hoylake anchorage two sets of leading lights were built on the Wirral Peninsula. The eastward ones at Leasowe were of brick and painted black and white, while farther to the west two towers were built at Hoylake. There were also, in 1766 when Williamson's chart was made, six buoys marking the banks on either side of the roadstead and the north side of the Rock Channel. The leading line for passing the Rock Channel, shown in Collins' earlier chart as two natural marks above Bootle, had been improved in 1766 by building two triangular timber marks above the Bootle shore and a stone beacon tower on the hill above. The Black Rock beacon perch which marked the turning point into the Mersey was enlarged and improved, and ultimately replaced by a lighthouse. Before that, a 55ft light tower had been built at Bidston, a village of the Wirral.

The Liverpool port authorities, later to become the Mersey Docks and Harbour Board, had always shown great initiative and their position was strengthened by the first Liverpool Pilotage Act of 1766. They were pioneers in dredging, channel marking and the enforcement of strict rules of pilotage. Their Wirral lights were soon converted to oil

Hutchinson's 1777 chart of Liverpool and Wirral anchorages. Note the newly established leading lights at Hoylake and Bidstone (labelled 'Sea Lights'), and the numerous buoys and other leading marks, (labelled 'Lake Lights'). (Wm. Hutchinson, A Treatise on Practical Seamanship*)*

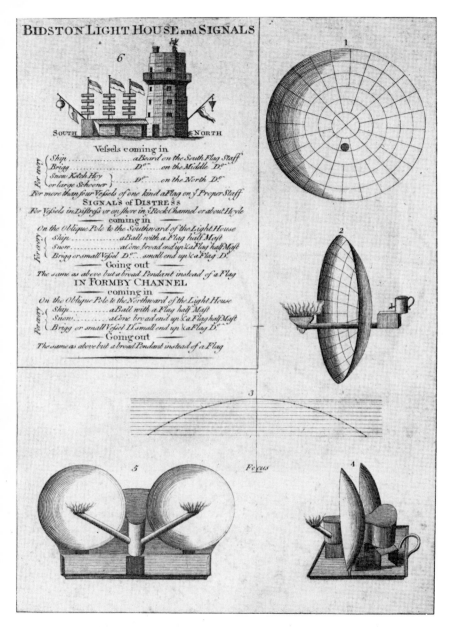

Oil lamps and parabolic reflectors as used by Hutchinson in his Wirral lights.

lamps with reflective enhancement. A quotation for building a lantern similar to one of theirs at Hoylake itemised a copper lamp at £2 12s 6d, a copper and tin enclosing pan at £8, and a looking glass with silvering at £14, which with other sundries added up to a total of £25. By the end of the century Liverpool had accumulated a lot of experience with catoptric lighting (see Chapter X) and the principles of parabolic reflection were better understood as a result of their efforts.

A plan for the Thames Estuary in the mid-seventeenth century shows the world's first lightship moored at the seaward end of the Nore

Bank which separates the Thames from the Medway, and two buoys had been moored at either side of the long middle-ground bank upstream of the Nore. Though these aids were supervised by the Trinity House at Deptford, more distant improvements were the work of local harbour authorities.

Local initiatives continued throughout the kingdom. A seventeenth century map of Jersey – one can hardly call it a chart – shows a stone cross on an above-water rock in the midst of the dangerous southeasterly reefs off the island. Early charts of the Little Russell Channel east of Guernsey showed that some of the well known marker rocks had been topped by pole beacons. The Rectors of Falmouth had been made responsible for maintaining an elm pole beacon on the Black Rock lying in the fairway. Such minor improvements for the benefit of local traders and fishermen were often paid for by local communities, but the Rectors were empowered by Parliament to take a toll of 6d from every decked ship entering their harbour.

In Scotland, the opening up of the Clyde harbours to the world's shipping had produced a host of navigational and hydrographic problems which the Glasgow magistrates and council were determined to overcome. They promoted an Act of Parliament which received the royal assent in 1756 and allowed them to build and to receive shipping tolls for a coal-fired light on Little Cumbrae, the small island which abuts the mid-channel approach to Port Glasgow. The local trustees built, manned and lit the light in just over a year, and they used the substantial surplus from the toll income to improve the harbour facilities and to maintain beacons and buoys in the most advantageous positions.

Liverpool, Glasgow and Hull can all, therefore, claim to have made substantial progress in dredging and marking their harbour approaches in the eighteenth century. The provision and maintenance of lights on the busy East Coast and in the Atlantic approaches, however, continued to be as much a matter of financial speculation as of public benefit. The Trinity House Corporations seem to have interpreted the provisions of their charters as entitling them to block or to modify schemes for coastal marking. The Hull Trinity House only succeeded after prolonged wrangling with landowners in getting leading lights established on Spurn Point, and as we have seen they had help from the Trinity House of Newcastle. Deptford Trinity House was increasingly used by the government and the Royal Navy as an advisory body who could supply marine experts to make local surveys, sound out local opinion and haggle with lighthouse proprietors.

By the eighteenth century Trinity House had yachts and tenders available to take the Brethren around on summer visits of inspection, especially to the East Coast where their Harwich depot was very active. The Corporation owned and manned some lights of its own, such as St Agnes and the pair at Lowestoft. After the great storm of 1770 when 40 ships had been lost in the vicinity, they embarked on a whole series of improvements including a system of multi-faceted mirrors revolving around an oil light for the front light of Lowestoft. This catoptric method of light enhancement, known as 'spangle lights' at the time, had a limited usefulness and a limited life as it was soon to be superceded by dioptric systems. It was, however, of great enough interest to attract a party of Trinity House Brethren to embark in their yacht to inspect the lights in 1778. Having looked carefully at the light at close quarters, they sailed out into the North Sea: then, approaching the coast by night, they were delighted to see that the new spangle light

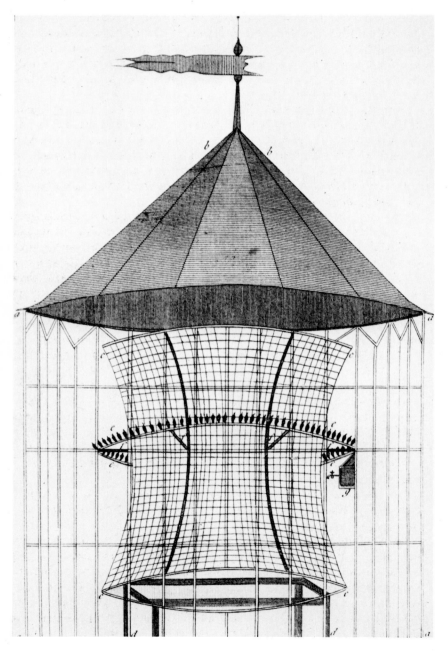

The spangle light at Lowestoft which gave the Brethren of Trinity House such satisfaction when it was lit in 1778. The concave drum was faced with 4,000 small squares of glass and the circular fuel line fed 126 lamp wicks. As it was expensive to build and maintain the design was not copied elsewhere. (Norfolk Museums Service)

was first visible at 20 miles while the coal-burning back light was not seen until they were 14 miles away.

The use of reflectors to concentrate the light from fires, candles and oil lamps had begun in Sweden in 1669 when the Landsort light was backed by a mirror. Other important advances followed. In 1681 King Karl XI gave a patent to J. D. Braun for his steel mirrors and in 1687 the Orskar light was fitted with reflectors. In 1757 the world's first flashing light was designed and fitted at Korsö by Norberg; two curved mirrors rotated back and forth by clockwork. Norberg also established the world's first revolving light at Marstrand in 1781; in this design the revolving reflectors were suspended from above and sent out a series of horizontal flash-beams. The importance of a parabolic curve on the reflectors was emphasized by Norberg, by Hutchinson of Liverpool and by Walker of Lynn.

The importance of giving lights distinctive characteristics was being generally recognized at this time, as a number of shipwrecks had occurred because the master had mistaken one light for another. At Cap de la Heve at the entrance to the Seine, two fire towers were built to show two fixed lights. On the Casquets north of Guernsey three fixed lights were shown, and in 1781 Trinity House ordered that these should have oil lamps and parabolic reflectors.

The end of the eighteenth century saw a tremendous upsurge of experiment and useful invention of methods of providing a safe and powerful light source and in concentrating the beam. By far the most significant was the Swiss invention, by A. Argand, of an efficient oil lamp with a circular wick. The Argand lamp with various types of fixed or revolving reflectors became the standard optimum light source by 1800. The publication of Hutchinson's *Treatise on Practical Seamanship* in 1777 also promoted the widespread use of parabolic reflectors. Ezekiel Walker of Lynn, a philosopher and physicist, who wrote many papers on optics and the sources of illumination, is credited with being one of those behind the early efforts to concentrate the beam by catoptric lighting. The leading marks on the Wirral Peninsula near Liverpool were first fitted with lights backed by a series of hollowed wood bowls lined with silvered glass facets, but Walker developed for them metal Sheffield-plated reflectors of parabolic shape. Walker's Hunstanton light had eighteen concave reflectors placed in such a way as to concentrate the beam of the light in the northeasterly sector where it was most needed.

Before the end of the century France had begun to advance rapidly in coast lighting and seamarking: there were 20 lighthouses operating by 1800.

Meanwhile, in America, the thirteen colonies under British rule had made their own arrangements for improving the entrances of their main harbours. In 1713 local merchants had petitioned the General Court of Massachusetts for a 'light-house and lanthorne' on some headland at the entrance to Boston. Eventually a lighthouse of sorts was built on Brewster's Island and tolls were charged for passing it. The lighting and administration were, however, fairly rudimentary and in

1751 a fire destroyed part of the tower. In 1775–6 it was several times damaged purposely by opposing forces in the War of Independence. In 1746 some rather weak beacon lights had been established at Brant Point by Nantucket Harbour, but they were frequently damaged by storms or out of action. In 1748 the first Southern light, a timber construction on Tybee Island in the approaches to Savannah, Georgia, was seen; and in 1764, Sandy Hook, New Jersey, which may be considered to be New York's first landfall light, was lit. It made history by being the first lighthouse to be financed by a lottery, the finances of New York city having ever been on a somewhat irregular basis! It was a substantial octagonal building with an iron and copper lantern burning 48 oil flames.

There were ten lighthouses of sorts built on the eastern seaboard, in the colonial era, but there was no attempt to set up any overall service either locally or nationally. Whale oil was used as lamp fuel, but catoptric methods of enhancement did not reach the U.S.A. until the next century. American lighthouse history after Independence will be described in later chapters.

Both greed and mercy had motivated the seamarking triumphs of the seventeenth and eighteenth centuries. On the one hand there seemed to have been a callous disregard for the dangers and discomforts suffered by the sailor and the lighthouse keeper, and on the other hand there was heroism, ingenuity and a readiness both to experiment and to apply the increasing knowledge of basic science. By 1800 the coasts of England were already better lit than the rest of Europe, though Sweden and France had already begun their rapid advance. As England was at war with France the Royal Navy began to take a hand in coastal surveying and channel marking. Scientific and engineering discoveries were making many things possible. Trinity House was building up a store of expert knowledge, providing facilities for experiment, and above all adopting a more public-spirited attitude. The scene was set for the great engineering advances of the nineteenth century which will be described in Chapter X.

Sources for Chapter VIII

G. Collins
D. Defoe
D. B. Hague and R. Christie
F. Ross Holland
W. Hutchinson
N. Long
C. Mair
R. W. Munro
C. Nicholson
J. S. Rees

IX

Lightships and Lanbys

The history of lightships compared with that of lighthouses, beacons and buoys is short. The idea of a floating guardship outside a harbour was an ancient one, but the suggestion that such a ship should carry a guiding light was first made in the seventeenth century. At that time, however, the problems of secure mooring and the protection of the lantern from wind and weather could not be overcome, so no permanent lightship was ever successfully deployed in those early years.

In 1731, David Avery, 'a gentleman of infinite projects', succeeded in outwitting the negative attitude of Trinity House and stationed a lightship close to the long-established buoy at the tail of the Nore Bank. The world's first lightship was a wooden sailing vessel which had been converted to carry twin candle lanterns. The Nore Bank is at the confluence of the Thames and Medway Rivers and lies some 2 miles northwest of Sheerness fort, so it was a key position for finding the entrances to the inner channels of both rivers. The fact that the Medway ports were then important naval bases was no doubt an important factor.

Avery had secured a patent for 14 years from July 1730 on the basis that his partner Robert Hamblin of King's Lynn had invented a method of making one lighthouse distinct from another. They purchased an old collier, after raising capital from several merchants, and stationed it close to the Nore Buoy maintained by Trinity House, thus angering the Brethren who had earlier advised that a lightship was not feasible. They were entitled by their Charter to a licence fee from all privately owned lights, but their financial rights to a new invention such as a lightship were uncertain: they appealed to the Admiralty only to find that the latter backed the two adventurers. After two years of litigation the Brethren got a revocation of the Avery patent, but by this time maritime opinion had swung round to support the Nore Lightship so a compromise was reached whereby Trinity House granted a lease to Avery at £100 a year for 61 years from 1733.

The Thames Estuary has very low-lying and marshy banks with extensive mudflats stretching out from both shores. It was difficult for an incoming vessel to fix her position accurately and the Nore buoy had for some hundred years served this purpose. Vessels making for the Thames or the Medway could not always time their arrival in the hours of daylight so a light, however weak, was of value in helping pilots to bring their vessels by night into the shelter of the rivers rather than being forced to anchor in the open estuary. The popularity of the Nore Lightship with sailors also helped Avery to achieve success in overcoming the hesitations of Trinity House; its profitability was an additional factor. On Avery's death they took over management of the Nore.

The candle lanterns were suspended from each end of a special yard on the vessel's foremast. The yard could be lowered to the deck so that the candles could be renewed and the lanterns cleaned. This method of cross-tree lighting was not suitable for a rough seaway, however, as the swinging of the mast and lanterns could put out the lights, cause a fire or waste the candles. To try to minimize jolting and swinging the bases of the lanterns were secured firmly by short lanyards or downhauls cleated at deck level.

It was wise of Trinity House to license their first light vessel in the comparatively sheltered inner waters of the Thames Estuary, for even there she was quite often driven off station by storms: it is possible that the lights were only shown consistently in summertime.

The experience gained by Trinity House led them to devise a mooring which employed two anchors set at right angles to each other and connected by a bridle attached by a heavy cable to the lightship's bows. This gave the greater holding power of two anchors while limiting the swing to less than on a single or tandem anchors. One of the crew's many duties was to pay out more cable in stormy conditions or in very strong tides. Each time they adjusted it they had to re-position a rawhide which was wrapped round where it passed through the fairlead or hawse pipe.

In 1736 a second lightship was stationed off the Dudgeon Shoal. The patentee was again David Avery who with associates in Great Yarmouth was constrained to pay a licence fee of £200 a year, rising to £300 after two years, to the Corporation. The Dudgeon Shoal lies on the direct collier route from Flamborough Head to Winterton Ness in Norfolk and is some 20 miles off the Lincolnshire coast. In this position the vessel was much more exposed than the one at the Nore. She parted her moorings many times in the first few years and was involved in several collisions. Again, twin candle lanterns were suspended from crosstrees, and the ship was equipped and manned in such a way that in the event of the cable parting the crew could sail her into port. The need for a light at the Dudgeon was so pressing that the licensees felt that, despite the risks, the lightship had to be kept on station for much of the year. She too was eventually taken over by the Brethren.

The difficulties with secure mooring and candle-lighting and the logistics involved proved so great the Trinity House was still not enthusiastic about lightships, however popular they were with seafarers. They responded reluctantly to pressure in 1788 and a vessel

A drawing of about 1800 showing the Dudgeon Shoals Lightship. This was similar to the first lightship at the Nore. Note the twin crosstree lanterns and the twin anchors with mooring bridle. (A. W. Lang, Geschichte des Seezeichenwesens*)*

was moored south of the Owers Bank, off the low-lying Selsey Bill and some 25 miles southeast of Portsmouth. This site was chosen because the Owers Bank was claiming an increasing toll of ships, some of them belonging to His Majesty's Royal Navy. The Owers was a classic lightship site where a dangerous shoal bank abuts a major shipping lane and where there is no high land near enough on which a sailor could fix his position. The needs of the Royal Navy and the increasing English Channel traffic inward bound from the Americas were sufficient to persuade the Brethren of Trinity House that they should venture another lightship. This time, however, they were able to equip her with the newly invented Argand oil lamp with its circular wick and protective glass chimney. The single circular lantern was hoisted up and down the short stocky mast so that the light's arc of visibility was somewhat obstructed by the mast itself. Logic decreed that a lantern should be designed which could not only be hoisted clear of the mast but be intensified by parabolic Sheffield-plated reflectors: a cluster of lamps needed to be used as a light source. No really satisfactory design emerged, but sufficient progress was made for Trinity House to station three more lightships before the end of the century. The Newarp Sand was lighted in 1790, and in 1798 the North Goodwins Lightship replaced a fixed beacon which had been driven into the sands with great difficulties and expense but which did not survive its first winter of storms. Three lights from oil lamps focussed by parabolic reflectors were shown at the angles of a wooden triangular frame mounted on gimbals. The last lightship of the eighteenth century was placed north of the Sunk Sand in a strategic position which commanded the fairways leading to London and to Harwich, Ipswich and Colchester. In 1798 and 1805, when there was a real danger of invasion by an armada of ships and troops massed on the Lowlands and North France coasts, plans were made to deprive the French of this invaluable mark, by taking the Sunk off station at short notice if they should move. All five eighteenth century lightships were so well sited that today there are still important lightships in the same positions.

In the early nineteenth century Trinity House continued to maintain its existing lightships and to improve the design of the oil lamps and lanterns, and three new lightships, the Galloper, the Gull and the Nab, were commissioned at the request and expense of the Admiralty during the Napoleonic Wars. During 1819 and 1820 there was a struggle between the Trinity Houses of Hull and Deptford over the stationing of a lightship to seaward of Spurn Point; Deptford wanted no risk and all the tolls. Hull finally went ahead without an agreement and at its own risk and expense, because the whole of East Coast maritime opinion was in favour, and Deptford received a heavy licence fee. The vessel was often holed by collision, driven off station and damaged, but despite these and major logistic problems her usefulness was never in doubt and she was a great financial success.

The English experience had been noted by the Dutch, the Germans, the French and the Americans, all of whom were aware of areas on their own coasts which could best be served by offshore lights. Between 1815 and 1818, after the upheavals of the Napoleonic wars were at an end, three lightships were stationed in the outer sea approaches to the Rivers Eider, Elbe and Weser. These ships were of sturdy construction and soundly moored. The light source was a complex wood and copper

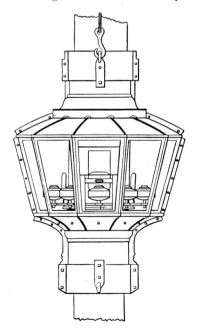

Robert Stevenson's design for a lightship lantern encircling the mast. It has ten oil lamps and ten glass panes but no reflectors. (A. W. Lang, Geschichte des Seezeichenwesens*)*

lantern which encircled the mast and was hauled up and down by tackle. In the lantern were five Argand-type lamps backed by parabolic reflectors to throw a mainly horizontal beam to all points of the compass. The French also celebrated the end of the wars by stationing a lightship off the Sandettie Bank north of Calais. Lightships then appeared off the Dutch coast, in the Bristol Channel, and off the eastern seaboard of the U.S.A. in the approaches to New York and Boston. The availability of chain cables from about 1820 made for the safety and reliability of lightships in more exposed positions. The most ambitious project of that period was the mooring of the Northeast Goodwins Lightship in the Dover Straits in 53m of water: this required 466m of chain cable attached to a 5 ton sinker.

In the nineteenth century lightships began to show riding lights as well as the main lights as it was found that this helped sailors to see which way the lightship was riding in the tide.

Lightships continued to use catoptric lighting after prismatic and spherical lens assemblies became available because the design and strength of the central mast would not allow a heavy superstructure. An English firm, Wilkins & Company, designed a twelve-lamp kerosene lantern backed by twelve parabolic reflectors. Wilkins lanterns were widely exported until, in the second half of the century, lightships adopted a lantern mounted on gimbals to minimize the swaying movements of the light as the ship was rocked about by the swell.

Later still, a central latticed tower replaced the mainmast, enabling a lantern to be constructed so that the lens assembly could revolve round the light source as in a fixed lighthouse. Thus the lightships of today are able to produce flash sequences comparable, except for range of visibility because of their height, to those emitted from lighthouses. Lightweight moulded glass optics, interspersed with blank panels according to the designated sequence, rotate on metal bearings. Secondary lighting in case of failure of the main light is in the form of battery powered sealed-beam lights fixed above the rotating optic; the character is the same although they may have a lesser range. During the twentieth century the main light source was gradually changed from oil lamps to electric bulbs powered by diesel generators.

A separate trend in the nineteenth century was the development of boat-shaped light floats in tidal rivers and estuaries. These are more

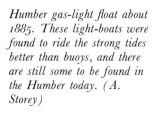

Humber gas-light float about 1885. These light-boats were found to ride the strong tides better than buoys, and there are still some to be found in the Humber today. (A. Storey)

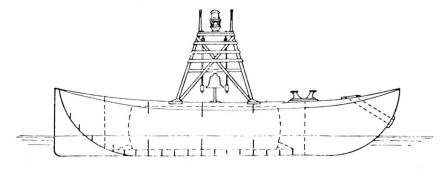

substantial than buoys and, except in the earliest years, unmanned. In the English Wash and the Humber they have been more serviceable than buoys at channel bends in strong tidal flows, as they can swing to the stream and lessen the strain on the mooring.

The lightship, situated as it usually is in or near the approaches to major estuaries or in the path of coastal traffic, has always been vulnerable to collision: many vessels and their crews were lost in the early years. Bells and horns were used in fog to warn passing ships, but when powered sirens, reeds and diaphones were later developed every lightship was fitted with such a fog signal, not only for self-protection but to guide ships up to the approaches to a channel or to fix their position by identification of the lightship which was always clearly marked with its name. As with light signals, care was taken to diversify the type of sound from lightships within the same area so as to minimize the risk of mistaken identity. Most lightships carry a Racon on their bow which transmits a range and direction signal visible on other ships' radars, in response to incoming radar. This serves both 'defensive' and position fixing functions. Many broadcast a radio direction finding signal; the transmitter aerial is slung between the foremast and the top of the central light tower.

An important change in the last thirty years has been the marking of seaways through constricted waters so that all the ships passing in a certain direction steer along a defined lane, separated from those on reciprocal courses by a 'separation zone' in much the same way as opposing streams of traffic on a motorway are kept apart to reduce collisions. At the entrances and exits of such separated lanes lightships may be strategically placed so that ships can 'home in' on them before altering course to enter the designated route. Since these points are often in quite deep water it is often thought to be appropriate to use a very large automatically lighted buoy instead of a light vessel. These are known as light floats in America where they were developed, but as large automatic buoys or Lanbys in Europe.

A Trinity House Lanby has a central pillar lantern standing some 15m above sea level and a circular railed deck beneath which are the sealed compartments. Access to these is through a waterproof door in the central pillar. In the lowest part of the buoy are three compartments to house separate diesel generators. One of these is engaged in generating power for the light, which shines by night and day, and the other two are standby engines which cut in automatically if the operating engine fails. The fog signal is electric. The operational state of the equipment can now be monitored telemetrically from a shore station. The Lanby is moored to its point of deepest draft and this gives the whole structure a very unpleasant, jerky movement in a seaway. Repair and maintenance of equipment is difficult if not impossible in these conditions. Lanbys are often damaged by collisions.

For these and other reasons, Lanbys are not regarded as a success by Trinity House whose present policy is to convert many of the existing lightship hulls, most of which are in very good condition, into fully automated vessels. These are equipped with three diesel electric

A Large Automatic Navigation Buoy (Lanby) as used by Trinity House.

A Telemetry aerial
B Racon
C Main and Standby lights
D Emergency light
E Bearing light
F Anchor light
G Fog signal
H Emergency fog signal
J Intake and Exhaust ducts
K Entrance door
L Equipment hatches
M Fuelling hatches
N 3 point Mooring lugs
P Mooring chain

Height of focal plane
above water line.................12.2 metres
Diameter of hull...................12.2 metres
Depth of hull.........................2.3 metres
Weight of buoy :— Empty ....55 tonnes
Normal water ballast ....25 tonnes
Max. fuel load ....15 tonnes
Total ....95 tonnes

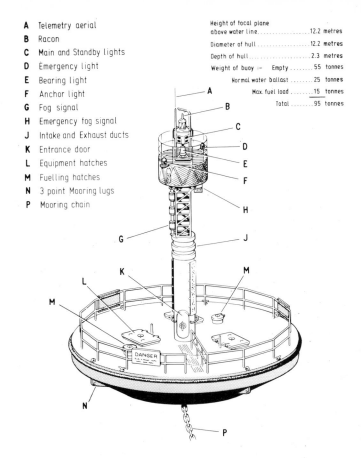

DANGER

A Lanby used by the Commission des Phares et Balises.

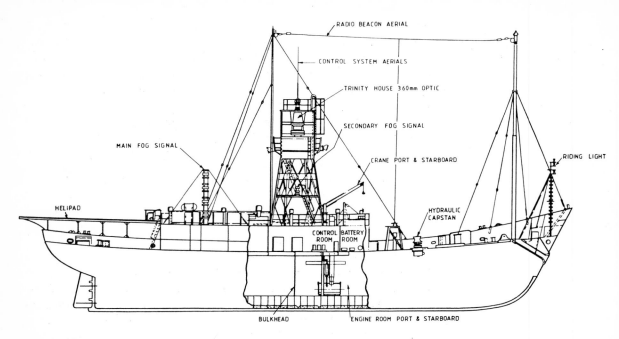

RADIO BEACON AERIAL

CONTROL SYSTEM AERIALS

TRINITY HOUSE 360mm OPTIC

SECONDARY FOG SIGNAL

MAIN FOG SIGNAL

CRANE PORT & STARBOARD

RIDING LIGHT

HELIPAD

HYDRAULIC CARSTAN

CONTROL ROOM BATTERY ROOM

BULKHEAD

ENGINE ROOM PORT & STARBOARD

generators, a diesel air compressor for fog signals, and a small power unit for the cable winch and bilge pumps. Such ships are liberally endowed with secondary lights and backup equipment so that at least two separate and unconnected failures have to occur before there is any danger of the light being extinguished. All automatic lightship functions are continuously monitored by telemetry by a manned shore station. Shock recorders and bilge monitors register collision or hull damage. The crew of a manned lightship often adjusts mooring cable scope (length) according to tide and weather conditions, but since this cannot be done on an automated ship she is moored to the centre of a bridle between two 3.5 ton Byers anchors set at 180° to each other. The ship therefore swings within the radius of both anchor chains, and moves less over the ground. Her exact position is monitored ashore by Decca: minor movements due to tidal change can be detected as well as any significant shift calling for emergency action.

At the time of writing (1985) Trinity House maintains eighteen manned lightships in British waters – more than any other European authority; ten Lanbys, two light floats and three automatic lightships. The programme of gradual and progressive automation of lightships continues, as is also seen in other maritime countries. Due to the problems encountered in the maintenance of Lanby equipment it is possible that some of these too will ultimately be replaced by the larger and more sophisticated automatic lightship.

Sources for Chapter IX

D. B. Hague
D. B. Hague and R. Christie
A. W. Lang
A. Storey

X

Lighthouses and the Age of Engineering The Nineteenth Century

Just before the end of the eighteenth century there began a rapid change from old haphazard ways and the piecemeal provision of seamarks. A more modern conception led to engineering solutions being found to the problems, both of illumination and of building lighthouses in remote situations. This is not to say that the eighteenth century lacked its pioneers and its heroes of seamarking. As we saw in Chapters VII and VIII, the early English experience of building lighthouses on rocks and reefs, especially the remarkable knowledge gained at the Eddystone, with its Winstanley, Rudyerd and Smeaton towers, had been assimilated by both the savants and the practical men of action who came later to be known as engineers. The successful maintenance of lightships near the dangerous offshore shoals of England, and the widespread European expertise in setting leading lights to help the passage of ships over bars or through dangerous channels, had prepared the minds of seafarers for further advances; indeed, they clamoured for better lighting of the coasts in numerous petitions. What was lacking was the organization to supervise, and the will and funds to pay for, the building of lighthouses, and also the application of already known physical laws to the science of illumination.

The French Revolution of 1789 acted as a catalyst for rapid change: many thinkers were energized by a new vision of the future, and logical minds were applied to the problems of coastal navigation. These factors, together with the widely felt need throughout Europe for better sources of light for lighthouses and leading marks, provided the necessary stimulus. Argand's oil-fuelled lamp with its circular wick and protective glass chimney had become available before the end of the century. It is probably true to say that this single invention, together with the later use of an incandescent mantle, changed the face of lighthouse engineering, as it changed the domestic lives of those who could afford to buy and use the new lamps. A new oil industry grew up based mainly on colza oil (manufactured from rape seed), whale oil was in equal demand, and the way was prepared for the eventual use of cheap mineral oils.

The science of optics grew throughout the seventeenth and eighteenth centuries, under the influence of the increasing demands of astronomy and microscopy. The properties of light and the laws governing its emission, diffusion, reflection and refraction were beginning to be well understood. In such an atmosphere of expanding basic knowledge, it was natural that scientists and 'ingenious men' of all sorts should address themselves not only to light sources but also to the means of concentrating light into a beam. As we have seen, Norberg of Sweden, Walker of Lynn and others saw the solution mainly in reflectors. Such catoptric enhancement of the light from an Argand lamp by parabolic reflectors of silvered glass or burnished metal was the best that could be devised, until Augustine Jean Fresnel invented his compound lenses which employed both prisms to reflect and spherical lenses to refract and so concentrate the beam of light. The brilliant French scientist was swiftly co-opted to the newly formed Commission des Phares in Paris and his experiments and inventions were immediately confirmed and taken up by the great lighthouse engineers of England and Scotland and later in the USA.

At this point in the story it is appropriate to review the history of French seamarking, because the central administration of Phares et Balises, which had its origin in a law passed in 1792, only three years after the storming of the Bastille, was a prototype for lighthouse organization throughout the world.

The coasts of France had seen primitive fire towers erected by the Romans near Boulogne and Marseilles, and the tower of Corduan in the mouth of the River Garonne was a typical example of the combined fortification and navigational aid which was sporadically built in medieval Europe. In subsequent years, monastic orders such as that at St Mathieu between L'Ouessant (Ushant) and Brest built and serviced primitive lights, so that by the time of the Revolution France had a number of lights and lanterns built and maintained by local communities. As in England, the locals were perhaps more interested in establishing their rights than in new developments. All that changed with the Revolution: the law of 1792 ruled with Gallic clarity that the Minister of Marine should be responsible for the surveillance and maintenance of '*phares et balises*' while the Minister of the Interior was to be responsible for building new lights where required. They were enjoined to co-operate.

Probably they did not do so effectively, and in any case the Parisian power struggles of the early revolutionary days would not have provided the right background for such technical improvement. Nevertheless, we find that the Ministers of the Interior had set up a directorate of Ponts et Chaussées before the end of the century, which had as its fields of activity roads, ports, bridges, canals and navigational aids. The growth of licenced privateering from centres such as St Malo and Morlaix, and the humiliations inflicted on the French fleets by the English at the turn of the century, must have focussed the attention of Napoleon's scientifically minded advisers on the necessity for good sea defences and seamarking if enemy ships were to be outwitted and losses of French cargos and vessels were to be reduced. In 1806 an Imperial decree vested all existing *phares et balises* in the Minister of the Interior, with the exception of the lights at St Mathieu, Ile d'Ouessant and Ile de Groix which remained the responsibility of the Minister of Marine. These exceptions were probably made with a view to the defense and security of both the main French fleet based at Brest, in the approaches to which lay St Mathieu, and of the French East India Company base at L'Orient outside which lay the Ile de Groix.

In 1811 the Director General of Ponts et Chaussées took the first steps to set up a Commission des Phares, the object of which was to utilise scientific advances, promote engineering experiments, and if possible standardize the methods of lighting for all the lighthouses around the coasts of the Empire. It was a broadly based Commission with representatives from the Academie des Sciences, the Ministry of Marine and the defence establishments, as well as a core of specialists from Ponts et Chaussées.

Thus, with force and logic, and with the help of Napoleon's formidable band of scientific advisers, the French lighthouse service embarked on a programme of research and development under unified control. It soon recruited to its councils that great physicist and engineer Augustine Fresnel, who had been trained in both the École Polytechnique and the École des Ponts et Chaussées. He died young, in 1827, but he had already made several fundamental contributions to the theory of light and had given the world the Fresnel compound lens assembly for lighthouses. He was recognized throughout the world and not only was he elected a member of the Academie de Science, but also a fellow of The Royal Society in London. He became the Secretary of the Commission des Phares soon after joining it, and after his death his brother Léonor continued his advisory work on lighthouse optics.

The Fresnel inventions were rapidly adopted and adapted by the Scottish father and son partnership of Robert and Alan Stevenson, who themselves invented numerous practical improvements to light mechanisms. The former did not have the benefit of these at the time he installed the lantern of his pioneer Bell Rock lighthouse, but the importunings of Sir David Brewster, an early advocate of lens lighting, caused the first Scottish Fresnel lens light to be installed at Inchkeith in the Firth of Forth. Alan Stevenson, having visited the ancient tower of Corduan which was the first French lighthouse to adopt the Fresnel system, installed a similar lantern at Skerryvore when it was completed in 1844.

The great leap forward in lighthouse building which took place in Scotland resulted from three major forces. The first was the enormous growth of the American sea trade. Ships following the great circle route approach the British Isles from the northwest and the natural advantages of the Clyde harbours were soon recognized and exploited. Nearby coal and iron mines made it easy for Glasgow to become within a few decades one of the most important shipbuilding ports in the world. The second force was the foundation in 1786 of the Northern Lighthouse Trust, later incorporated as the Commissioners of the

Profiles of the five Eddystone lighthouses with their dates of completion. The helipad on the present-day structure was added in 1980. (Trinity House)

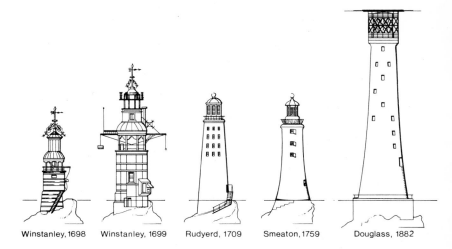

Winstanley, 1698   Winstanley, 1699   Rudyerd, 1709   Smeaton, 1759   Douglass, 1882

Northern Lighthouses, an independent Scottish body which owed something to Trinity House experience but without its charitable and other responsibilities and interests. Because, like its French equivalent, it was conveniently centralized, the task of marking the sea coasts of Scotland proceeded rapidly and efficiently after the Trust was freed (in 1789) of the necessity to obtain an Act of Parliament for each light. The third and driving force behind Scotland's lighthouse building was the character and ability of Robert Stevenson and his family. He was a brilliant and practical engineer who kept up to date with scientific advances throughout the world, contributed many himself, and was determined to find solutions to the huge engineering problems of building lighthouses on rocky coasts and exposed offshore reefs.

The structural problems of rock lighthouses had been demonstrated by the eighteenth century experience on the Eddystone and the Smalls. The consensus of opinion in England, France and Scotland was that Smeaton had got it right; there was no substitute for a system of building which used shaped masonry blocks dovetailed into each other both laterally and into the courses above and below. The towers had to withstand forces of up to 3 tons to the square foot so that cement binding alone would not stop the blocks from shifting. The huge weight of the masonry tower was in part its own safeguard provided that the shape put the centre of gravity low down and central, and that the surrounding rocks broke the force of the waves sufficiently to prevent them climbing up the tower.

In order to husband the skilled labour force on the lighthouse rock the numbered stone blocks were shaped and fitted exactly together on shore. The number of hours during which it was possible to work on an exposed and wave-washed site in the early building stages was necessarily small: it is estimated that fifty summer days with an average of five hours in which tide and weather would allow was the most that could be worked. This meant that in a whole year only 250 hours of work was possible on the rock itself, so that not only was the most meticulous planning called for but nearby shore establishments had to be set up with quarries, jetties, cranes and housing. The workboats and barges carrying stone, masons and blacksmiths had to be towed out to the site at the correct state of tide; many hundreds of hours were lost when the weather changed for the worse before or after the work force was landed on the rock. The experienced engineer had to learn to make contingency plans to maintain the productivity of his workforce throughout a protracted spell of bad weather. As steam-powered paddle vessels came into service less time was wasted on passage between shore base and rock, and so life was both safer and more comfortable for the rock workers.

The table gives a list, by no means exhaustive, of the major rock lighthouses built in the nineteenth century, from which can be seen that, after the pioneering work of Stevenson on the Bell Rock in the second decade, the number of rock stations increased exponentially, reaching a peak in the 1870s. The chief engineering problems faced by Stevenson and Rennie at the Bell Rock were: (1) How to secure a sound and flat base for the tower; (2) How to minimise the time wasted in transporting men and materials to and from the site; (3) How to facilitate the unloading of stores and masonry blocks at the rock.

Their solution to the first problem was to send out a team of skilled blacksmiths and sufficient equipment to keep the stone-cutting tools sharp and in good repair. The second problem, with its important financial implications, was met by chartering a substantial vessel which could be moored near the rock and act as a barrack for the workforce

The scene in July 1811 when the Bell Rock tower was almost completed. Note the barrack, the elevated iron railway from the landing places and the bridge between barrack and tower.

who were resting between tides, being treated for injuries, or who had to leave the rock because of weather or darkness. The Stevensons also constructed separate barracks and stores on a raised superstructure some 70ft above the sea, both at the Bell Rock and at Skerryvore. Each of these barracks, which took more than a year's work to build, was based on nine iron piles driven into the rock and secured together by a network of cross-members. Once the barrack was completed it became possible for key members of the workforce to remain on site for the whole day and so to utilise every possible hour of low water.

The third problem was solved at the Bell Rock by building an iron railway from the landing point to the base of the tower. Because the Bell Rock was just the highest point of an extensive sandstone plateau, the site lent itself admirably to this solution, and although the railway was submerged every high tide it was so soundly constructed that it continued to be useful at lighthouse reliefs until recent times. At Skerryvore, priority was given to the building of a jetty and lifting gear at the best landing point.

The overriding consideration for any lighthouse builder from

Lighthouse relief at the Bell Rock making use of Robert Stevenson's old iron railway, which at the correct state of the tide provides a good landing and unloading facility. (C. Nicholson, Rock Lighthouses of Great Britain*)*

Smeaton onwards was how to build the tower so that it could resist the immense destructive force of storm-driven waves, and the waterborne boulders which were often flung against it. Smeaton's solution was followed with modifications. The granite blocks were shaped to templates at the onshore building site by skilled masons: one 2 ton block could require 250 man-hours to complete. Each block, with its lateral, superior and inferior dovetailing, had its own individual shape and dimensions according to the master plan. The onshore workforce also had to include many skilled draftsmen and carpenters. In order to cope with the second problem they first designed and built templates, so that the masons ashore could be steadily employed in shaping the stones. As each stone was completed it was numbered and laid aside until a trial course could be laid at the yard. The numbered stone had to be correctly placed and then had to be levered and wedged until its dovetails fitted neatly with its neighbours. Only when all possible snags had been identified and corrected, when the trial course was found to be perfect, and when weather and transport allowed, was the stone despatched to the embarkation point.

At the site, the stone was lifted into position with tackle and cranes and carefully wedged up to lock with its neighbours. So intricate were the dovetailed joints, designed as they were to withstand enormous disruptive forces, that there was only one direction from which a new block could be levered into its final position. The last masonry adjustments, which had to be made with great care so as not to break or damage the essential locking keys, were completed and a final seal was achieved with a specially prepared cement. Trenails, marble dowels and wedges were also used to bind stone to stone and course to course.

The final constraint on the lighthouse engineers was that of cost, but we are surprised, when reading the history of those exciting times, to find how little such considerations seemed to impede the plans of the

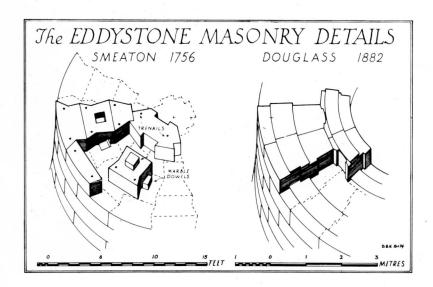

Masonry details from Smeaton's and Douglass' Eddystone towers. (D. B. Hague)

pioneers, especially after the idea of a temporary light was proposed, to allow tolls to be charged to help raise funds during construction of the main light. Labour was cheap and skilled, the engineers had faith in themselves and their workforce, and their financial backers had sufficient foresight and belief in the future of shipping not to subject their men of genius to financial harassment. We are surprised at the amazingly low costs of works which often took five years or more from planning to completion and employed at peak periods more than two hundred men. The cost of a project had to include the finding and opening up of quarries, the building of workshops and jetties, and the charter or purchase of work vessels. In the case of the Stevensons' projects, costings were generally very accurate and overruns rare.

Let the pen of Robert Louis Stevenson, the son and nephew of successive engineers to the Northern Lighthouse Board, describe the scene at Erraid on the Isle of Mull, when the Dubh Artach lighthouse was being built 14 miles out in the Atlantic in 1870.

'There was a pier of stone, rows of sheds, railways, travelling cranes, a street of cottages, an iron house for the resident engineer, wooden bothies for the men, a stage where the courses of the tower were put together experimentally, and behind the settlement a great gash in the hillside where granite was quarried. In the bay, the steamer lay at her moorings. All day long there hung about the place the music of clinking tools . . . In fine weather, when by the spyglass on the hill the sea was observed to run low upon the reef, there would be the sound of preparation in the very early morning; and before the sun had risen

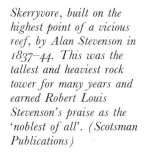

Skerryvore, built on the highest point of a vicious reef, by Alan Stevenson in 1837–44. This was the tallest and heaviest rock tower for many years and earned Robert Louis Stevenson's praise as the 'noblest of all'. (Scotsman Publications)

from behind Ben More, the tender would steam out of the bay. Over 15 miles of the great blue Atlantic rollers she ploughed her way, trailing at her tail a brace of wallowing stone-lighters. The open ocean widened upon either board, and the hills of the mainland began to go down on the horizon, before she came to her unhomely destination and lay-to at last where the rock clapped its black head above the swell, with the tall iron barrack on its spider legs, and the truncated tower, and the cranes waving their arms, and the smoke of the engine-fire rising in the mid-sea . . . .'.

Three thousand miles to the west the young but burgeoning United States of America had been struggling with the problems of lighthouse administration and procurement and were just beginning to emerge from their first period when poor leadership, corruption and local inefficiency had combined to make the service universally despised. Soon after the Declaration of Independence Congress had passed an Act in 1779 which gave responsibility for all aids to navigation to the federal government. The actual administration was devolved on the Secretary to the Treasury, who personally supervised the first few years of the Lighthouse Service; between then and 1820 it was either under his direct supervision or his Commissioners of Revenue. In 1820 the service came under the control of the Fifth Auditor of the Treasury, Stephen Pleasanton. He had an unhappy association with a Mr Lewis, who was involved in commercial companies supplying the lighthouse service as well as acting as his technical adviser. Lewis's advice seems often to have been wrong, or at worst directed by his own commercial interests. Thus, it was not until the second decade of the eighteenth century that catoptric lighting was adopted in the USA, and the appliances for which Lewis had been granted a patent proved to be circular rather than parabolic, and thus much less efficient than others of that time. Furthermore, keepers had been instructed to clean the reflectors with an abrasive mixture which progressively damaged their surfaces. No proper tests of luminous efficiency were made, and keepers and superintendents were often political appointments.

All this sorry story came out in 1851 when Congress appointed an investigating commission composed of a scientist sitting with naval and military specialists. Congress had already sent Commodore Perry to Europe to study Fresnel lenses, and had also set up an Inspectorate on the eastern seaboard which was divided into six districts. The basic weakness in the service, however, was not really remedied until the report of the investigating commission in 1851 led to legislation in 1852. This set up a proper lighthouse service with a controlling board which included not only most of the investigating commission but others with professional and scientific qualifications.

Despite the evident inefficiency of the service up to 1852, there were in that year already 331 lighthouses, 42 floating lights, 35 beacons and over 100 buoys along the vast coastline of the United States. During the second half of the century, the engineering achievements of the Lighthouse Service were outstanding, with several wave-washed rocks and underwater shoals and reefs successfully marked and lit, though not without difficulties. The very first light on Minots Ledge in Massachusetts was a nine-legged pile structure which was destroyed by a gale in 1851; fortunately the keeper had taken refuge ashore. It was replaced by a stone tower in 1860. On the Pacific seaboard, by fantastic efforts Gibbon and Kelly managed to build a dozen lights on the Californian and Oregon coasts within four years, even though their supply ship was wrecked in the mouth of the Columbia River. Alcatraz Light in San Francisco harbour, which they began in 1852, was first lit in 1855.

Still farther west, in the China Sea and the waters of the Indies, it appears that seamarking was not an indigenous skill. All the developments which took place in the second half of the century were forced ahead by the pressure of colonial penetration.

While the Stevenson family dominated Scottish lighthouse engineering for the whole of the 1800s, the Douglasses, grandfather, father and son, had the same influence on the projects which Trinity House undertook in English and Welsh waters, mostly in the latter half of the century. They achieved some remarkable feats of building with the Wolf Rock, the second Bishop Rock, the Longships and the (fourth) Eddystone. In some ways these Cornish sites were more difficult than the Scottish ones. Most of the southwestern rock towers were built on isolated rock pinnacles, which were only clear of the sea at low water on calm days: in the early stages of site preparation and fixing the foundation courses, a season of 250 working hours was all that could be hoped for. Working area was very restricted and there was not room to construct a barrack. The workforce had to live on board the workboats, or in the case of the Bishop on a nearby bleak, windswept island. Due to these natural handicaps and the collapse of the first iron tower, the second Douglass took more than seven years to complete the first

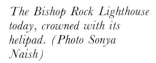

The Bishop Rock Lighthouse today, crowned with its helipad. (Photo Sonya Naish)

Phare d'Ar'men, which took fourteen years to build and is the most westerly rock lighthouse in France. (Commission des Phares et Balises)

Bishop Rock granite tower. The Wolf tower took eight years, but the fourth Eddystone, which required a coffer dam for its foundations, only four. In France, Reynaud and Allard faced an equally daunting assignment in trying to erect a tower on the submerged rock of Ar'men west of the Isle de Seine. It was not only wide open to the full force of the Atlantic, as were the Cornish offshore sites, but was also swept by 6 knot tides that ripped across a line of underwater rocks stretching out from the island like a finger pointing to the New World. The tower took 14 years to complete; there were 290 landings and 1,217 hours of work on the site.

In Britain some order had been brought into the administration and financing of lighthouses. Impelled by the complaints of seafaring interests objecting to the multiplicity and cost of private lighthouse tolls, and no doubt shamed by the progress being made in Scotland and France by centralized administrations, Parliament set up a select committee chaired by Joseph Hume to look into the administration and technical management of lighthouses and other forms of seamarks throughout Great Britain. The work of this committee, though its report was not unanimous, led to the President of the Board of Trade presenting a Bill to Parliament which resulted in the passing of the Lighthouse Act of August 13, 1836. This left the Scottish and Irish Lighthouse Boards to continue work in their own areas of jurisdiction, though it gave Trinity House a general supervising function, with a view to the limitation and equalization of tolls and the monitoring of the need for new and costly capital works. Buoyage and minor or very local lights were the responsibility of the local port Authorities such as those administering the Mersey, Clyde and Tay: they took the risks and collected harbour dues in return. However, their plans had to be submitted to Trinity House for approval. Its most important feature was the vesting of all private lighthouses used ·by the generality of shipping in English and Welsh waters in the Corporation of Trinity House. Funds were voted for Trinity House to purchase these lights; this they did, but at considerable cost, during the succeeding decade. The income from the tolls so acquired proved sufficient for the major capital improvements in England, Scotland and Ireland during the next 50 years, and for a beginning to be made in buoyage, daymarks and minor lights not directly in the entrances to ports.

In 1894 the Merchant Shipping Act, as amended, constituted a General Lighthouse Fund from which all the authorities in the British Isles drew their income. The principle was adopted, which has continued to this day, of levying tonnage dues on voyages made where lights and other aids were used, rather than on the number of lights passed.

In 1830 Alexander Mitchell of Ireland had invented the Screw-Pile system of driving iron legs into sand or shingle. The Maplin Sands light, with its nine wrought iron legs screwed into the sand, was successfully built and put into commission in 1836 and other screw-pile structures followed in England and Ireland. The coasts of Germany,

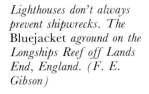

Lighthouses don't always prevent shipwrecks. The Bluejacket *aground on the Longships Reef off Lands End, England. (F. E. Gibson)*

A model of the Maplin Sands Light, built on nine Mitchell screw piles in 1848. (Science Museum, London).

Holland and the USA were in many ways suitable for the screw-pile system for lighthouses, but where the submerged sands were too deep and the tidal scour too strong some more substantial method was required. As we have seen in Chapter III, the navigational hazards outside the great North German rivers consisted mainly of shifting shoals and the lack of recognition marks. When in 1881 a light was planned for the approaches to the Weser, an earlier English experience of sinking a caisson beacon into the submerged sands off Reculver in the Thames Estuary was drawn upon. The difficulties facing the German engineers were, however, of a different order: not only was it required to base the Rothersand tower on shifting sands some 20ft below low water level, but the tidal scour was severe and continuous. The first

The Rothersand caisson under tow to its final position. (F-K. Zemke)

steel caisson was sunk to 70ft below low water; during the process scouring caused it to tilt alarmingly, but it was hoped to get it stabilised in the following summer. However, the first winter storms undermined the structure and it collapsed. Two years later, in 1883, a larger and differently shaped caisson was sunk to a depth of 73ft, then reinforced on the outside by iron plating. Internal sand was removed by suction and the cavity filled with concrete, while stones and mattress work were used to bolster the outside.

The Americans followed with two similarly constructed caisson-concrete towers on submerged sandbanks in Chesapeake Bay (Wolf Trap) and Delaware Bay (Fourteen Foot Bank). Previously the Americans had built a masonry rock tower on Minot's Ledge and, under very great difficulties, a masonry tower on a submerged reef off the California coast (St George's Reef) in 1891. The coral reefs of Florida called for different solutions: the method chosen was to drive iron piles into the coral and then build an openwork iron superstructure surmounted by a lantern and living quarters 80ft above the sea. Several such lighthouses were built off the Florida coast, and the British used similar techniques to place the iron lighthouse on the Daedalus Reef in the Red Sea.

Except in tropical and subtropical waters where submerged coral reefs were the main navigational hazard, the iron lighthouse was never successful in exposed situations, however. The first Bishop Rock tower of cast iron was destroyed by storm before the lantern was installed and a similar attempt on the Fastnet Rock in southern Ireland was a failure. It was gradually accepted that cast-iron lighthouses, though cheaper than masonry, were not suitable for exposed sites. A good many were built in harbours or on secure headlands, however, throughout the world.

Lighthouse engineering was an established branch of civil engineering by the end of the nineteenth century, with its own corpus of knowledge and experience. Engineers trained in Great Britain and France were never short of employment in the rest of the world. The coasts of India, Australia, New Zealand, South Africa and the French Colonial Empire were being provided with lights at those places which seafarers had found to be the most critical, and a great deal of resourceful experiment was needed to overcome the difficulties of transporting materials to remote sites. Meanwhile, the science of optics had made great strides; the manufacture and working of special glass for prisms and lenses were being undertaken by elite firms in France and England. Better methods were also found for rotating the lens assemblies around the light source in such a way as to provide flashes, continuous light or occultation as local circumstances demanded. The problems and uses of coloured beams, holophotal lights and differential sector beams were being explored.

Before starting to describe nineteenth century achievements in applied optical illumination, it is first necessary to introduce some of the principles and terms which have to be used in describing these developments. Rays of light may be concentrated by reflection (as from mirrors) or by refraction (as in lenses). The prism may be used either as a refractor or as a reflector, depending on its shape and the angle at which the ingoing beam of light strikes it. Simple reflective systems using parabolic surfaces are known as catoptric systems. Reflecting prisms which do not reverse the light beam but only change its direction acutely are known as catadioptric, while a spherical lens is an example of a dioptric system.

The essential feature of Fresnel's thinking was that he sought to use every available photon. He therefore assembled lenses and prisms in such a way that the light was concentrated in the vertical axis, no rays being wasted in searching the sky or lighting up the floor of the lantern chamber. The available systems of illumination were categorized into classes which are still used. Class I is a horizontal beam of light directed

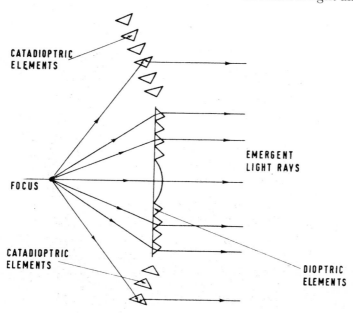

The Fresnel lens profile (International Dictionary of Aids to Marine Navigation)

to all parts of the compass. Class II, a horizontal beam further concentrated into flashes perceivable over a certain area for a fraction of a second and then revolving round the horizon to reappear at its original point after a defined time lapse (period). This is perceived by the mariner as a flash recurring (say) every 10 seconds while a dimmer light can be seen continuously when closer to the light. In Class III a beam of light remains concentrated in a certain bearing or arc. Such a beam is known as a holophotal beam and the lights emitting them are usually called sector lights. They are particularly useful at close quarters when beams of red or green can more readily be perceived, and can either warn of dangers or indicate a clear channel through them.

In order to achieve the characteristics of these three classes of concentrated light, the engineers had first to find some reliable means of revolving the optical assembly around the light source, and they had to be sure of both quality and accuracy in the manufacture of optical components. The former was easier to achieve than the latter. The first revolving system was installed at Marstrand in Sweden in 1783 and used a catoptric system of reflectors suspended from above. Similar apparatus was installed in the Corduan lantern in 1790, at Flamborough Head (using red glass to give an alternating red and white beam) in 1806, and a more sophisticated version incorporating fog bells at the Bell Rock in 1811. The reflectors were mounted on a carriage revolved by a clockwork mechanism, the weights of which had to be wound up regularly by the keepers. After Fresnel's discoveries a revolving dioptric system was first adopted by the Commission des Phares and then taken on by Alan Stevenson, who installed them at Inchkeith and the Isle of May. By the time Skerryvore was lit the system used had been greatly improved.

At this early stage the only source of precision-worked optical glass was the French manufactory of St Gobain, but later Messrs. Cookson of

The light source and Fresnel lens in the North Forelands fixed sector light.

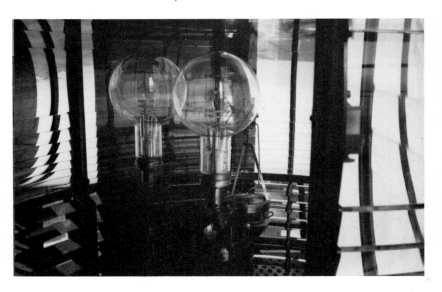

Newcastle in England took over as the sole suppliers of the Fresnel assemblies. They were advised by the inventor's brother, Léonor Fresnel. Later in the century, Letourneau & Lepaute of Paris and Chance Bros. of Birmingham became the specialist suppliers to the world. Catadioptric lens and prisms assemblies such as are still used today did not become available until after 1850. As the weight of the lens assemblies increased, it became impractical to suspend them in the manner of the first catoptric systems. Lubricated rollers were used to support the heavy dioptric and still heavier catadioptric assemblies.

As the number of lighthouses increased, it became more and more important to diversify the flash patterns (character of the light) so as to diminish the chance of one light being mistaken for another. A light flash every five or seven seconds could easily be mistaken for one every ten seconds, so care was taken by the various national authorities to give neighbouring lighthouses quite distinct periods and flash characteristics. The permutations were few, however, despite the fact that some lights were steady and others occulting, while those needing only to be seen from relatively short distances might be red or green. The Casquets light had since the mid-eighteenth century showed three separate lights to make sure that it could not be mistaken for any other. Because of this problem, more acute with the growing number of lights around the coasts, Robert and then Alan Stevenson compiled the first ever List of Lights, published as *The British Pharos* in the 1830s. It was a complete list of all coastal and harbour lights in the British Isles, describing their appearance by day and night; an elegant and essential tool for navigators who after a period of bad visibility or being blown about by gales might easily be very uncertain of their position. Charts were expensive and not necessarily up to date or sufficiently detailed. Similar Light Lists are still produced today by the maritime authorities for the risks and consequences of mistaking seamarks remains.

Systems followed which allowed a group-fishing sequence to be emitted. Groups of two, three, four or even five flashes could be produced, thus greatly increasing the variety of signals within a given area and lessening the chance of mis-identification. Such quick flashing sequences demanded an increased speed of rotation, at which friction on the bearings became an important limiting factor. Towards the end of the century Bourdelle hit on the brilliant idea of floating the whole assembly, weighing several tons, in an annular bath of mercury. Owing to the enormous density of mercury, a quantity of the liquid metal

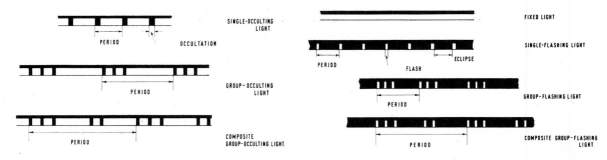

weighing perhaps 100kg could support a lens assembly of 3000kg. The drag or friction was minimal; the vast lighthouse lantern could be revolved by the touch of a finger. The mercury bath system cut down wear on the parts, and the work of the keepers who had to wind up the weights for the clockwork.

Thus, as the nineteenth century came to an end, the design and engineering equipment of the lighthouses had reached such a state of reliability that the first half of the twentieth century saw few important changes. Mineral had replaced colza oil because it was both cheaper and more reliable with incandescent oil lamps. Electricity was being used extensively in onshore harbour lights, as was gas, but early British experiments with steam-generated electricity at the South Foreland lighthouse had not been successful enough to make most authorities abandon oil, which had proved over the years to be reliable, cheap and easy of maintenance. In a later chapter the move towards electric lighting of major lighthouses in the second half of the twentieth century will be described.

The new iron and steel technology had made possible, directly or indirectly, the greatest feats of civil engineering. Among the bridges, the railways, the first skyscrapers, we must place the lighthouse which, though built of precisely designed and worked stone, required all the sophistication of steel tools, cranes, rails and attendant ships for its successful completion. They are probably the most highly stressed of land structures, and the pinnacle of heavy-masonry building. The triumphant acceptance of the challenge of working in the desperate conditions of a wave-swept rock represents a pinnacle of Victorian engineering achievement.

The ability of those Victorian engineers to face such problems with confidence was only matched by the confidence of the workers in their chiefs, who often shared the discomforts, the dangers and the terrors of the masons and labourers in a leaky barrack on an Atlantic rock in a Force 10 storm. Very few lives were lost or serious injuries sustained because the engineers were canny and cautious men who knew that there was no place for guesswork in such circumstances of danger. They must have known also that the success of their enterprise would depend on maintaining the morale of their workers and checking panic before it could spread. This is why, on reading the accounts of builders like Alan Stevenson, we find next to nothing about labour troubles. Complaints must have been as strident as in any other group of humans, but they were dealt with humanely or else sublimated in the adventure of co-operative achievement. The Stevensons were also humane to a remarkable degree; concerned not only with the welfare of their workmen and lighthouse keepers, but of the dependents who survived those who died in the service.

Diagrammatic representations of light characters. (International Dictionary of Aids to Marine Navigation)

Phare de Kéréon off Quiberon, built in the late 1800s. The photo shows the fierceness of the tides. (Commission des Phares et Balises)

Longships Lighthouse with helipad. (Trinity House)

Sources for Chapter X

E. Allard
H. M. Denham
G. M. Elliot
Encyclopaedia Brittanica (11th Ed); Lighthouses
D. B. Hague and R. Christie
F. Ross Holland
C. Mair
R. W. Munro
C. Nicholson
J. S. Rees
M. L. Reynaud
D. A. Stevenson
F.-K. Zemke

Dates of Building	Location	Site
1759	England, Eddystone	Wave-washed rock
1807–11	Scotland, Bell Rock	Wave-washed rock
1823	Ireland, Haulbowline Rock	Wave-washed rock
1836–39	France, Heux de Brehat	Wave-washed rock
1838–41	England, Maplin Sand	Submerged sand
1840	England, Wyre, Fleetwood	Submerged sand
1838–44	Scotland, Skerryvore	Wave-washed rock
1854	Ireland, Fastnet	Isolated rock
1854	Singapore, Horsburgh·	Reef
1849–53	France, Haut Banc du Nord	Reef
1853	Ireland, Spit Bank, Cork	Submerged sand
1847–50	England, Bishop Rock	Wave-washed rock
1851–58	England, Bishop Rock	Wave-washed rock
1855–60	USA, Boston, Minot's Ledge	Reef
1856–61	England, The Smalls	Wave-washed rock
1861	France, Biscay, Bayes d'Olonne	Wave-washed rock
1862	Guernsey, Les Hanois	Wave-washed rock
1863	Red Sea, Daedalus Reef	Submerged reef
1865	India, Bengal, Alguada Reef	Submerged reef
1869	England, Wolf Rock	Wave-washed rock

ıtlying Lighthouses

Type of Construction	Cost	Outcome
Masonry	£40,000	Replaced 1882
Masonry	£55,619	Successful
Masonry	Unknown	Unknown
Masonry	Unknown	Successful
Screw pile with superstructure	Unknown	Discontinued
Screw pile with superstructure	Unknown	Survived
Masonry	£72,200	Successful
Cast iron plates	Unknown	Unsuccessful, replaced
Masonry	Unknown	Successful
Masonry	Unknown	Successful
Screw pile with superstructure	Unknown	Survived
Cast-iron openwork	£12,500	Destroyed in storm
Granite masonry	£34,559	Rebuilt 1887
Masonry	£62,500	Successful
Masonry	£50,124	Successful
Masonry	Unknown	Successful
Masonry	£25,296	Successful
Iron superstructure on screw piles	Unknown	Successful
Masonry	Unknown	Successful
Masonry	£62,726	Successful

Dates of Building	Location	Site
1872	Scotland, Dubh Artach	Isolated rock
1872	England, Longships	Wave-washed rock
1870–73	Sri Lanka, Great Basses	Reef
1870–74	USA, Huron, Spectacle Reef	Reef
1878	Sri Lanka, Little Basses	Reef
1875–78	USA, Florida, Fowey Rock	Reef
1880	USA, Florida, Alligator Reef	Reef
1867–81	France, Brittany, Ar'men	Submerged rock
1881–85	Germany, Rothersand	Submerged sand
1885–87	USA, Delaware, Fourteen Foot Bank	Submerged sand
1893–94	USA, Chesapeake, Wolftrap	Submerged sand

Type of Construction	Cost	Outcome
Masonry	£72,584	Successful
Masonry	£43,869	Successful
Masonry	Unknown	Successful
Masonry cone (to withstand ice)	£78,000	Successful
Masonry	Unknown	Successful
Iron piles and superstructure	£32,600	Successful
Iron piles and superstructure	Unknown	Successful
Masonry	£32,692	Successful
Caisson, filled by concrete	£65,000	Successful at 3rd attempt
Caisson, filled by concrete	£24,700	Successful
Caisson, filled by concrete	Unknown	

XI
The Search for International Uniformity

Towards the close of the nineteenth century, when the greatest engineering triumphs of that age had already been completed, attention began to be directed to the inconsistencies in the marking of the sea by buoys and beacons. Three factors contributed to the urgency of the problem. The first was that the improved durability and visibility of rivetted iron buoys had already led to their being moored farther out to sea, where their identity and significance was not so immediately ascertainable by the mariner approaching from seaward. Second, the number of buoys had increased exponentially over the last decades of the century. Third, the greater speed of the steamship called for rapid identification of marks and correct orientation of the ship in relation to them. Without these, the master or pilot was liable to steam over the dangers which the buoys were set to mark.

Two distinct categories of buoy identification had developed over the years, one based on colour and the other on buoy shape and topmarks. The latter was more certain in poor visibility, but colour was useful when there was a profusion of buoys and beacons in narrow and winding channels. As we have seen, the original tonne buoy was perforce black with tar or pitch, but experiments with white, red and striped colours had been made in the eighteenth century. White easily became stained and obscured, while red was not easily appreciable at such at a distance. The tonne or barrel buoy had also developed either as a cone with base upwards or as a spindle-shaped nun or spar buoy pointed at both ends. Sailors found that a tapered, pointed top was fairly easily distinguishable, from a flat-topped buoy at a distance, so the two shapes were often used to denote opposite sides of a channel. As iron buoys came into service, it was much easier to build them in distinctive shapes and to crown them with topmarks. Thus, in most seafaring countries the flat-topped buoy with a can, square or cylindrical topmark was becoming differentiated from the conical buoy with a tall topmark which was either triangular or diamond-shaped.

By the middle of the 1800s there was already a good deal of confusion throughout the world as to the accepted meaning of topmarks, but a consensus was gradually emerging that the flat-topped or 'can' buoy, as it came to be known, should be used as a port-hand mark for vessels entering harbour while the spindle or conical buoy with pointed topmark should be used on the starboard hand. The Mersey Docks and Harbour Board, which was one of the earliest authorities to develop a coherent buoying strategy, was a notable dissentient from this general consensus and many future difficulties flowed from this difference. There was also a deep division between the authorities and nations that favoured a red colour for starboard-hand marks and those who preferred it for port-hand. The grounds for the latter point of view, which seem to us now to be much more logical and weighty than they did at the time, were that the ship's port navigation light, being red, would 'match' the red-coloured buoy lying to port. Since the Collision Rules, the navigational 'rule of the road', decreed that ships on reciprocal courses should pass each other with port-side to port-side ('red to red' at night), it seemed logical to oppose the red port-side navigation light to the red port-hand buoy. Furthermore, since ships kept to the right side of a channel, and when meeting, it was also logical to use red as a danger sign for the left or 'wrong' side of the channel when entering harbour. It was assumed that ships leaving harbour, which had of course to keep close to the 'red' side of the channel, would find less difficulty than those entering, perhaps for the first time.

The Mersey Docks and Harbour Board of Liverpool, which had been very active in both dredging and in channel marking, had unfortunately developed a uniform system of its own in which red was the colour for starboard-hand buoys and black for port. Due to Liverpool's initiative and its close trading connections with America and other British West Coast ports, the authorities in the USA and Scotland adopted the Liverpool system. The Irish authorities adopted the opposite colour code. Trinity House, with jurisdiction and influence over most of Southern England and the British colonies, favoured whole colours, either black or red, for starboard and parti-coloured marks for port

This is how matters stood before 1880, but meanwhile it was becoming clear that a purely lateral system of buoyage in which a ship was assumed to be making for or leaving a harbour would not be adequate for the increasing number of buoys which were being laid to mark outlying dangers such as shoals and submerged rocks. In these wider waters vessels were on passage and not necessarily either entering or leaving harbour. This dilemma led to the development of a cardinal or compass-point system of marking for buoys in the open sea. Russia and Finland had improved on the old idea of birch besoms as topmarks pointing up or down to denote the north or south side of a channel. All Baltic nations were confronted with geographical conditions (numerous islands, islets and rocks all along the coast) which precluded the use of a lateral system except in the approach channels to harbours at the heads of fjords or in river estuaries. In the first place there was no tide, and a prerequisite of the lateral system was that the ship was presumed to be either entering harbour or proceeding with the main stream of flood tide. In the second place, the comparatively shallow channels between ports were often marked the whole way so that at no point could a ship be said with certainty to be entering or leaving harbour. If a purely lateral system of buoyage was used, then at some arbitrary point the buoyage direction would have to be changed.

These constraints led to the early use of the cardinal system in the Baltic, the Black Sea and, to a certain extent, in the Mediterranean. France was swift to adopt the cardinal system on both its Mediterranean and Atlantic coasts for outlying buoys and beacons, though the lateral system was retained for the marking of large rivers and the entrances to major ports.

The cardinal system as it developed relied on the use of conical or triangular topmarks to indicate where a danger lay, and on vessels having compasses. For example, a buoy or beacon with its cone or triangle point up could be placed to the north of a danger within the quadrant bounded by the compass bearings NE and NW; such a buoy is known as a north cardinal buoy as the danger or obstruction lies to the south of it. Similarly, a topmark with point down was a south cardinal mark. East and west cardinal buoys had two cones, with their points or bases together. Unfortunately, no universal rule existed and some countries used points together for east while others used points together as west.

The other new development in the 1880s was the lighting of buoys with gas-fuelled flashing lamps. It thus became urgent to agree on what flash sequences should be adopted for port and starboard buoys.

These new developments and the increasing speed, draft and tonnage of screw-propelled steam vessels provided the background to the Trinity House conference of 1882–3, held in London under the presidency of the Master who was Queen Victoria's son, HRH The Duke of Edinburgh. It was there resolved that for those waters under the control of the Trinity House the following conventions should be adopted:

Starboard Hand marks:	Conical shape with staff and globe topmark
Port Hand marks:	Flat-topped can with staff and cage topmark
Middle Ground, Bifurcation or Junction marks:	Spherical with horizontal stripes
Recognition or Landfall buoys:	Pillar (spar) with vertical stripes
Wreck buoys:	Green

No firm recommendations were made about colour to denote laterality except that starboard-hand buoys should be invariably unicoloured. It is interesting that there were two dissident opinions from the majority report of the conference. Bayly of Trinity House objected on the grounds of the expense of replacing the buoys in the Thames Estuary, while Thomas Stevenson of Scotland was far-sighted enough to question the wisdom of establishing uniformity solely on the basis of a lateral system and had wanted the conference to go straight for a cardinal system.

At this stage there had been several international maritime conferences, but none were of sufficiently broad national representation or depth of organization to achieve worthwhile results in the matter of sea-marking until the International Maritime Conference of 1889, held in Washington. This conference, which was convened in an atmosphere of increasing urgency caused by the explosive growth of sea traffic and the rapid technical progress both in ship propulsion and sea lighting, did succeed in achieving a reasonable consensus. The importance of moving towards international uniformity of buoy shapes, topmarks and light sequences was recognized. From this date, it also seems to have been generally accepted that there had to be both a cardinal and a lateral system of buoyage, that wreck buoys had to be clearly distinguished from other buoys, and that channel or landfall approach buoys should be of pillar form and sufficiently tall. It was also recommended by the conference that starboard-hand buoys would be conical, have pointed topmarks and be painted in a uniform colour. Washington went further in recommending the use of red for starboard and black for port, but it was conceded that white or parti-coloured buoys could be used to port.

In the same year, 1889, a conference of those concerned with maritime works and engineering had been held in Paris at the time of the Great Exhibition. It set up a permanent commission based in Paris, charged with the duty of preparing future conferences for those involved in developing harbours, breakwaters, docks and navigational aids. Before this date an international organization with a regular programme of conferences had existed for the purpose of coordinating inland navigation. It took nine years of negotiation before the maritime and the inland navigation organizations finally combined in the Permanent International Association of Navigation Conferences (PIANC). For this reason the first PIANC conference which dealt with coastal navigation aids was number eight in Paris in 1900. The headquarters of PIANC was established in Brussels.

The importance of ensuring that lighthouse lights should not be confused one with another had long been recognized by the various national lighthouse authorities, who had co-operated with each other with regard to lights near national boundaries or in international seaways. It was generally accepted that lights of similar character should be separated by at least 40 nautical miles. The question of a code for lighted buoys was also a subject of concern at the end of the century. The preferred solution was to use even numbers for starboard.

On the question of buoy colouring in the lateral system, there were unfortunately irreconcilable conflicts of opinion. The adoption of the Liverpool, and later Washington, system with red to starboard was finally recommended to all participating nations, but although some European countries (notably France, Italy, Portugal, Holland and Belgium) later adopted the Washington code, the then most powerful shipping nation of the world, Great Britain, was loath to adhere. A

Trinity House Conference of 1891 did go so far as to advise the eventual adoption of the Washington code, but with the important proviso that the change should not take place unless a significant number of other nations adhered to it. In spite of the fact that a majority of the Western European nations had agreed to conform, the British Board of Trade vetoed any moves to change the British system of buoyage, which was not even uniform throughout the British Isles. Scotland adopted the Liverpool (Washington) system quite early, and the unfortunate Commissioners of Irish Lights were constrained to change their port-starboard colour code twice in twenty years. The Mersey Docks and Harbour Board continued to use their preferred system of buoy colouring (which conformed with the Washington recommendations) and their buoy shape code (which did not) well into the twentieth century.

Early in the twentieth century there were regular conferences of the increasingly inflential PIANC; the ninth was held in Dusseldorf in 1902 and the tenth in Milano in 1905. PIANC 11, held in Russia at St Petersburg in 1908, lacked British representation, and the participating nations made the astonishing decision to reverse the Washington recommendations on colour and thus to promote red as the colour for all port-hand buoys. Italy, Spain and Portugal decided to adhere, so that by the time of the First World War there was a notable lack of uniformity in the buoyage system of Europe. Those parts of the world which formed part of the British Empire or were under the predominant influence of British shipping interests had in general followed Trinity House practice. Apart from the red-black controversy and the British use of particoloured buoys to port, there was then not a great deal of difference between the conventions followed in the British and the American spheres of maritime interest. The latter extended to Japan, the Phillippines, much of the Pacific and both Central and South America.

At PIANC 13 in London in 1923 the first consultations took place on the idea of setting up an informal organization of the heads of Lighthouse Authorities. This bore fruit at PIANC 14 in Cairo, 1926, when there was the first gathering of the heads of many important Lighthouse Authorities. It was resolved that regular meetings would be held in the future, to be called 'Informal meeting of the representatives of Lighthouse Authorities. The next such occasion, known as the London International Lighthouse Conference of 1929, was an important turning point as it secured, under the chairmanship of Mansell, the effective co-operation of the heads of most Lighthouse Authorities and those working under them who were concerned with visual, sound and radio navigational aids. There was, of course, a great deal more to harmonization than the shape and colour of buoys, but the latter remained an intractable problem world wide.

The League of Nations now took a hand, and its Advisory and Technical Committee for Communication and Transit produced a draft agreement which was initialled by all of the participating nations, but due to the long period allowed for consultations and discussions at national level, and the intervention of the Second World War, the agreement was never ratified though it was followed by many countries subsequently. The draft was a landmark in being the first attempt at a binding international agreement. It is also notable as having come down firmly in favour of red as the best indicator of port-hand marks. This decision reflected the growing European consensus that it was more logical to use red as the signal for left side of a channel when red was already used to denote the left side of a ship. The mnemonic 'there's red port left' had won over 'red right returning' in Europe – but not in America and in those vast areas of the world which were and are under American maritime influence. The Americans' case, made to the League of Nations Committee in 1931, that throughout the world there were more 'red right' buoyage systems than the reverse was a strong one. This is the root reason for the final, present IALA concord being qualified by a division of the world into two distinct regions, in one of which system A applies and in the other system B.

After the Second World War the thrust towards international co-operation on all matters nautical and aeronautical was strengthened by the rapid 'shrinkage' of the world due to speedier methods of travel and communication, and also from the increasing danger of accidents by collision. After preparatory work by the Fourth International Lighthouse Conference in Paris in 1950 and the Fifth Conference at Scheveningen in 1955, the International Association of Lighthouse Authorities (Association Internationale de Signalisation Maritime) was set up. In 1965 they appointed an international technical committee to examine the problem of a uniform international system of buoyage and to suggest solutions. The work of this committee was far more important than anything that had gone before, and it was pursued with great vigour. Thirty-one countries were involved in the working groups; more than forty committee meetings were held in the fifteen years from 1965 to 1980, and almost as many working group meetings. A genuine wish for uniformity motivated the participants from all nations. In contrast with the frustrating delays of the past, progress was rapid.

In 1976 IALA, backed by IMCO (the International Maritime Consultative Organization), now known as IMO, had reached basic agreement on a uniform system of buoyage, to be known as the IALA Maritime Buoyage System A, which was to be introduced forthwith in Europe, Africa, Australasia and the western half of Asia. In 1980 the representatives of fifty countries and nine international organizations, including IALA, IMO and IHO, finally agreed on worldwide adoption, with an agreed line of demarcation between the two regions A and B in which the two systems were to operate. By 1981 all participating nations had agreed to incur the expense of putting the new systems into operation. The change of buoys and beacons is proceeding rapidly, along with the consequent changes to charts, Light Lists and other hydrographic publications, and seems to have won a wide measure of approval from seafarers.

Sources for Chapter XI

Board of Trade, England 1933: Historical Notes on Uniform Buoyage
E. P. Edwards
IALA, 1982: International Co-operation in Aids to Navigation
1889–1955.
IALA Maritime Buoyage Systems 1980
N. F. Matthews
Report of the Royal Commissioners, 1861, London
Report of the Conference on Uniform System of Buoyage for the
United Kingdom, 1883.

Some International Bodies and Congresses Concerned with Fixed Navigational Aids

English	French	Acronym (s)
Permanent International Association of Navigation Congresses	Association Internationale Permanente des Congres de Navigation	PIANC (AIPCN in French)
International Technical Lighthouse Conferences	Conférence des Services de Signalisation Maritime	CSSM
International Association of Lighthouse Authorities	Association Internationale de Signalisation Maritime	IALA (AISM in French)
League of Nations Advisory and Technical Committee for Communication and Transit		
International Maritime (Consultative) Organization	Organisation Internationale Maritime	IMO (previously IMCO) OIM
International Hydrographic Organization	Organisation Hydrographique Internationale	IHO OHI

Significant Conferences on Seamarking 1882 to 1980

1882–3	London	Trinity House Conference	Seeks uniformity in British Isles: fails
1889	Washington	International Maritime Conference	Promotes Liverpool system for buoyage
1891	London	Trinity House Conference	Advised adoption of Washington code only if sufficient nations adhered. Board of Trade later vetoed adoption. France, Italy, Holland, Belgium and Portugal adopted Washington code.
1900	Paris	PIANC 8	
1902	Dusseldorf	PIANC 9	
1905	Milan	PIANC 10	
1908	St Petersburg	PIANC 11	Reversed Washington colour code to Port = Red. Britain not represented. Italy, Spain, Portugal adhered.
1912	Philadelphia	PIANC 12	
1923	London	PIANC 13	
1926	Cairo	PIANC 14	
1933	Paris	International Technical Conference on Lighthouses etc	
1936	Geneva	LNATCCT	Draft Agreement for international system of buoyage included Port = Red. Never ratified by participating nations, but adopted by some after World War II.
1937–8	Berlin	CSSM 3	
1950	Paris	CSSM 4	
1955	Scheveningen	CSSM 5	
1965		IALA	Sets up international technical committee to examine problem and suggest solutions.
1976		IMCO	Agreement in principle on System A.

1977	IALA	Introduction of System A in Europe, Australia New Zealand, Africa and part of Asia.
1980	IMCO IALA	Representatives of 50 Countries and 9 international organizations agree to adopt new rules and the boundaries between Regions A and B.
1981	IMO	Whole world begins to conform to IALA system.

XII
The IALA System

The Association Internationale de la Signalisation Maritime (AISM), which is known throughout the English speaking world as the International Association of Lighthouse Authorities or IALA, has its headquarters in Paris. The French, with their centralized system of lighthouse administration, have always been active in seeking international uniformity of seamarking, so it is thus thoroughly appropriate that Paris should be the headquarters of this important body.

As we have seen, the Second World War prevented the world-wide adoption of the Uniform System promoted by the League of Nations in 1936, but as countries began to re-lay and renew their buoyage following the devastation of that war, there was a general tendency to adhere to its recommendations. Nevertheless, there were more than thirty different systems of buoyage in use throughout the world even as late as the 1970s, and the final agreement on an international system must be regarded as a triumph of common sense over the worst form of conservatism. The expense and difficulty for small nations conforming to the international system will surely be recouped by future savings in equipment procurement and by the real but hardly quantifiable benefits of greater safety for ships and those who sail in them, their cargoes and the marine environment.

The general principles of the IALA system are very simple and are based on usages and codes of shape, colour and lighting which have over the years gradually been accepted by the seafaring community as sensible and easy to understand. It applies to fixed and floating marks but not lighthouses, sector lights, leading lights or marks, Lanbys or lightships. Five separate types of mark are recognized: Lateral (or channel) marks; Cardinal marks, used in conjunction with a compass; Isolated Danger marks; Safe Water marks, i.e. landfall and mid-channel marks; and finally Special marks which are used for features such as pipelines and other obstructions, recreation or traffic areas, the nature of which can be seen by reference to a chart, sailing directions or Notices to Mariners (channels reserved for deep-draft ships are another instance).

New Dangers are defined as those not yet charted or notified, and are marked by one of the first four types above according to the local navigational requirements. Such buoys are often duplicated until the danger is charted and well recognized.

Due to the long-standing preference and usage by the Americas for the colour red to denote right or starboard hand, the world has been divided into two regions. In Region B, which includes most of the Western Hemisphere plus Japan, Korea and the Philippines, red buoys and red flashing lights are left to starboard when entering harbour or proceeding in the Conventional Direction of Buoyage. In all other respects, such as buoy shape, topmarking and the use of stripes, Regions A and B are identical.

Lateral marks are planned to be 'read' as by a ship presumed to be entering harbour or proceeding along the Conventional Direction of Buoyage as indicated by the national authority. These conventional directions are based on two assumptions: first, that a vessel entering harbour with the main flood tide is presumed to be travelling in the conventional direction, and second that in coastwise sailing the conventional direction is clockwise around large land masses. (Under IALA the British Isles are now classed as large islands within the general clockwise flow around the continent of Europe.) Vessels travelling in the conventional direction leave starboard markers to their starboard side and port-hand markers to port. Where channels divide the preferred channel is marked with modified, horizontally banded, lateral marks which indicate by their shape and topmarks which way deep-draft ships should proceed. Thus, in Region A, port-hand marks are red, of cylindrical, pillar or spar shape, flat-topped and have topmarks with a square silhouette. Lights when fitted are also red. Where channels divide, the preferred channel port-hand marks have a horizontal green band across the red; lights are red. Starboard hand marks are green with green lights and have a triangular point-up topmark, and can be of conical, pillar or spar shape. Preferred channel starboard hand marks are also green with green lights, and a horizontal red band. Both kinds of preferred channel mark have a distinctive (2 + 1) flashing rhythm not used by any other.

In Region B the lateral colour codes are the reverse of those in Region A, though the buoy shapes and topmarks are identical. Port-hand buoy lights in Region A are red, starboard hand ones are green: in Region B this usage is reversed.

Cardinal marks are yellow and black, and usually pillar or spar shape. They indicate by their colouring, topmarks and light rhythm in which direction the safe, deepest water lies. All topmarks are double black cones and all lights are white. Because cardinal marks are positioned in one of the compass quadrants, to know where they are in relation to the hidden danger they mark the user must have a compass, a requirement unique to this type of mark. The double cone topmark allows four different configurations, each denoting a compass quadrant; the yellow and black colours on the buoy itself also convey this information, but may not be as unambiguous in some sea conditions. The quick or very

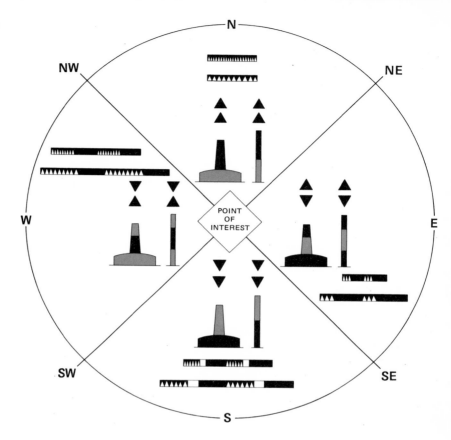

quick flashing light is specific to cardinal marks and by its rhythm shows the compass quadrant.

We have seen how during the last hundred years the round topmark and horizontal banding came to symbolize a *middle ground* or *isolated danger* in otherwise deep water. IALA has settled on red and black horizontal bands as the code for such hazards, which can be passed on any side. The topmark is two black spheres one over the other. If buoys can be moored over the obstruction they are of the pillar or spar type, but if, as is frequently the case, it is surmounted by a perch or masonry beacon, the same red and black bands and two round topmarks are used. If lit, such marks show a white flashing (2) light. Where neither a fixed structure (beacon) nor a floating one can be placed on or over the danger, for example because the mooring chain would become fouled by it, a mark has to be placed farther away and then a different type, usually cardinal, has to be used. This is the case with wreck marks.

With the increasing demarcation of seaways where all ships are encouraged to travel on the same or nearly parallel courses, it is more than ever necessary to have a special type of mark to denote the 'central reservation' separating opposing lanes. In deep waters tall pillar or spar buoys with vertical red and white stripes and a single red spherical

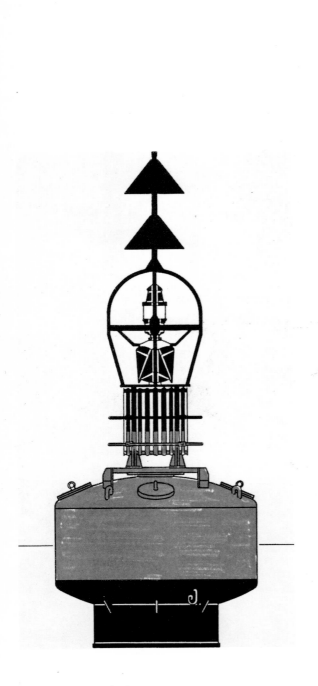
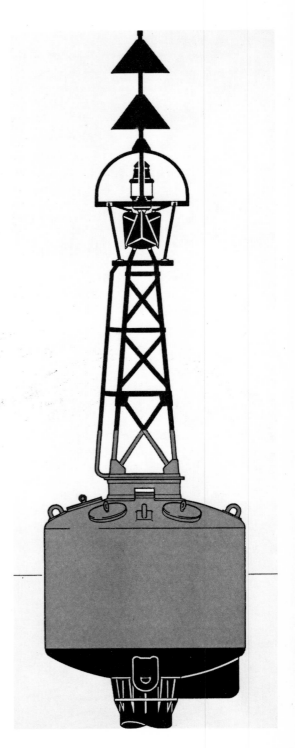

Two modern steel buoys, both prepared as North Cardinal marks. The skirt keel on the shorter buoy is clearly shown, but the long tail tube of the taller one has been omitted in the drawing. The light-coloured bottom part would be painted bright yellow. (Trinity House)

topmark are used. The light is white, either occulting, isophase or the short-long of Morse code A. *Special marks* are all-yellow buoys with X topmarks, of various shapes so designed as not to be confused with normal navigation marks. Their yellow lights are of any rhythm not likely to be confused with navigational lights.

The introduction of the IALA System began in Region A in 1977 and has already gradually spread throughout Europe, Australia, New Zealand, Africa, the Arabian Gulf and many Asian countries. In 1980 the rules for Region B were completed and the worldwide IALA Maritime Buoyage System was launched, with a few minor modifications of the rules for Region A in order to make the whole system coherent and truly worldwide.

As the IALA information document truly says: 'The IALA Maritime Buoyage System will, for the first time, help the Mariner of any nationality to fix his position and to avoid dangers without fear of ambiguity. This is indeed an important and positive contribution to the safety of life and property at sea.'

Sources for Chapter XII

Maritime Buoyage System (1980). International Association of Lighthouse Authorities, Paris
N. F. Matthews

XIII

The Automation of Seamarks

As the lighting of the coasts proceeded in the nineteenth century, it became clear both to the lighthouse authorities and to the seafaring fraternity that to set up a service capable of year-round function required something more than the casual employment of retired seamen, fishermen and even their widows, as watchers of lights and repairers of beaconage. We have seen how the Trinity House organizations, the Commissioners for Northern Lights and the expanding Port of Liverpool sought to carry out their hydrographic, dredging and seamarking functions by employing permanent staff, which included scientists, marine surveyors and engineers as well as a devoted force of handy seamen. They set up shore depots and chartered or designed ships specially to service their buoys, beacons and lights. We have seen how post-Revolutionary France set up a centralized administration of Phares et Balises in Paris and how, by mid-century, most advanced nations had recruited a specialist corps of engineers and light-keepers.

Alongside this nineteenth century trend towards the growth of large staffs can be discerned the first attempts to make the illumination of seamarks more automatic. The most rapid change came in the last three decades of the century when the successful manufacture of metal buoys, screwpiles and cast-iron beacons introduced a new dimension. Such structures, which were useful as daymarks, also required lighting, but they were too small to support a large lantern or to house keepers. Those countries whose coasts were encumbered with rocks and islets were the ones most interested in developing automatic lighting, and thus we find that it was in Sweden, with its vast indented coastline, that the Trotter-Lindberg automatic light was invented. This light was fuelled by petroleum spirit stored in cisterns and could be maintained by regular visits. After it had been tried and found satisfactory in Sweden, it was installed at a single site in the Thames Estuary.

As reports were favourable, the Commissioners for Northern Lights in Scotland decided to adopt the system on an experimental basis. Already, the authorities there had agreed to follow a policy of building minor lights, after the Secretary of State for Scotland had accepted a report, in 1890, from a committee which had taken evidence from the fishing industry and the scattered communities of the Western Highlands and Islands. Scotland, with an abundance of islands, sheltered sea lochs, deep sounds and straits through which deep-draft ships could pass safely if forewarned of isolated dangers, was, like Sweden, ideal terrain for minor automatic lights. It also had then a thriving herring industry and a huge fleet of coastal carriers. The Secretary of State, responding to these pressures, reserved for minor lights and light-keeping a sum of money from that allocated to the welfare of the Highlands and Islands.

The Commissioners for Northern Lights already had some experience of automatic gas lighting because light buoys had been used in the Clyde since 1880. They chose as the site for their first fixed automatic light the Grey Rocks, which lie almost in mid-channel of the Sound of Mull. This was a very busy inshore route used not only by coasters and passenger vessels serving the Inner Hebrides, but also by fishing boats making for the railhead at Oban. The light on Grey Rocks was of the Trotter-Lindberg type and could be maintained and inspected by a specially trained local fisherman. The next such light was installed on the large but windswept island of Stroma in the

Dubh Artach Lighthouse with helipad, built on the site of Stevenson's building barrack. (C. Nicholson)

Pentland Firth south of the Orkneys. Shortly afterwards, in 1895, the Benson-Lee automatic lamp which burnt kerosene was adopted for all new installations. This was more easily maintained by semi-skilled men recruited from the local fishing communities. By the end of the century there were already twenty such minor lights in Scotland.

The marking of the Oxcars Rock in the Firth of Forth illustrates some of the changes leading up to automation. In 1846 an unlit stone beacon was built to replace a cast-iron beacon first erected in 1804. It was enlarged to a lighthouse in 1885, but due to cramped space and difficulties of manning the light was soon converted to automatic operation. The light source was oil gas, drawn from large storage tanks which had to be refilled from the local gasworks every two weeks. The keepers lived ashore nearby and kept an eye on the light which came on automatically at dusk. This was achieved by keeping a small pilot flame going throughout the twenty-four hours, while a clockwork mechanism, maintained and timed by the keepers on their regular visits, switched on the main light at sunset.

Between 1895 and 1910 ten more minor 'sound' lights were converted to automatic gas mechanism, with one keeper living ashore retained to service each of them. By 1914 and the outbreak of war there were 68 minor lights operating in Scottish waters, of which approximately a third burned oil gas, a third acetylene gas and a third kerosene.

Both the Scandinavian and the French authorities in the twentieth century have followed a consistent policy of automating suitable minor lights and of lighting their previously established beacon towers. Such French balises, built to withstand severe wave stress on the Atlantic coast, were often sufficiently large to accommodate fuel stores and small automatic lanterns.

The worldwide move towards automation has everywhere speeded up in the last 25 years under the impetus of new inventions such as the sealed-beam light assembly, electronic control devices and refinements in electricity supply. There has also been the negative force of escalating manpower costs as the conditions of human labour have improved.

As with so many nautical and navigational advances of the recent past, much is owed to the experience of the aeronautical industry. The chief directions of progress have been the following:

Automation of major lights with shore base monitoring by means of land lines or telemetry.

New sources of illuminant power, principally self-generated electricity from automatically operated diesels or wind power.

Smaller and more powerful light sources with shorter focal length optics, thus reducing the need for tall and bulky optical lens assemblies.

Light moulded glass and polycarbonate lenses which can often be built up from standard modules.

Maintenance of sophisticated apparatus by skilled engineers who make regular inspections by helicopter, whereas previously they went by sea.

Historical developments in light intensity from lit seamarks. (Modified from F-K. Zemke)

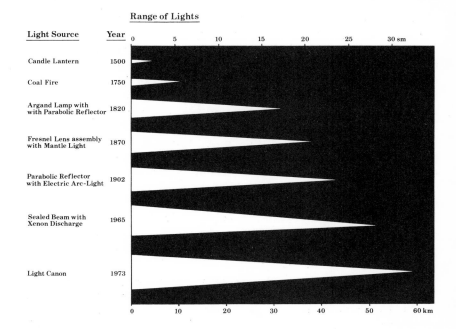

The building of helipads on or near lighthouse towers to facilitate relief of manned stations, refueling, and repair and maintenance of automatic stations.

The widespread use of radio aids and radar enhancement (racon) facilities from all types of seamarks.

The Swedish Lighthouse Authority under the brilliant guidance of the engineer Lennart Hallengren has pioneered a complete and controlled system of automatic lighthouses and beacons. The telescopic lighthouse has in some places replaced the moored lightship. Many beacons and minor lights have been connected by underwater cable to the mains electricity supply. The use of helicopters for expert servicing of distant automatic lights was so successful in the 1960s that other lighthouse authorities throughout the world were convinced by the Swedish experience that automation was coming in and ship-relief of manned stations was going out. The comprehensive automatic system of navigational aids is all centrally controlled at Norrköping. The operator there can not only monitor the functioning of lights, sound signals and radiobeacons but he can interrogate sensors of each system at each lighthouse. It is remarkable that the Swedish Navigation Aids Service, which controls some 90 lighthouses, 930 beacons, 300 lit buoys and thousands of spar buoys, is worked by less than 150 people.

The equipment and power requirements of the modern lighthouse have changed drastically since the end of the nineteenth century, most of the change having taken place since the Second World War. As a result of many scientific advances and the spin-off from techniques employed in the car and aeronautical industries, the power requirement of the light itself has been reduced to between a quarter and a fifth of that at the end of the nineteenth century. The luminous efficiency of the lights and optical systems has increased in parallel with the improved power efficiency. The main source of power is today either mains electricity supply, if feasible, or self-generated power using diesel alternator sets. Other power sources such as wind-generated electricity, photo-voltaic cells and even dry batteries are used in experimental sites, on buoys or lit beacons, or in special sites where geographical considerations justify such high capital cost installations. The main power source in rock stations and automated lightships being the diesel alternator, problems develop due to the more rapid deterioration of engines which stand idle for much of their life. Very often problems are encountered in starting a diesel engine after a period of inactivity, and this is more likely in a marine environment. The life of the engine is thus not simply a function of the number of hours of use. Much thought and research goes into overcoming this inherent problem in a service which must have back-up equipment standing idle, and the optimum schedule of use for any one engine has still to be agreed upon.

Many different types of light source have been tried in lighthouses. The xenon discharge flash, which has many theoretical advantages in that it is power efficient, small and reliable and has been tried out in major landfall lights, has not proved popular due to the fact that the very horizontally concentrated beam may not produce much of a 'loom'. Mariners rely a great deal on being able to see the loom of the light in the sky before they can see the flash itself. A very short though intense flash also introduces problems of orientation when seeking to take a bearing. The xenon discharge lamp and other similar light sources are most suitable for short-range lights and leading lights where a bright light by day and sharply defined beam are required.

The sealed-beam light backed by a parabolic reflector appears to have a good future, mainly for economic reasons. These units can be purchased relatively cheaply from manufacturers for the automobile and other transport industries. We find that the Trinity House light at Dungeness is emitted from a panel of sixteen 250W sealed-beam lights which revolves on a turntable and needs no lens assembly in front of it. It is about a tenth of the weight of the older glass lanterns. The sealed-beam units are identical with those used as headlights by American railway locomotives and can therefore be purchased at more economical rates than would be the case if they were custom built for a lighthouse service.

The tendency today is to use, if possible, equipment which has been developed for a larger market and then to assemble the units in a suitable manner. To illustrate this point, it has been found that the tungsten-halogen light as used in slide projectors is a suitable light source small enough to use a lens of 50mm focal length. An alternative arrangement would be to use a street lighting lamp, for example a mercury vapour discharge type, and to surround it with six lightweight lens panels of moulded glass and polycarbonate of 360mm focal length. The cost of the equipment would be low and also the cost of maintenance and replacement. Since the power and luminous efficiency of such a modular assemblage would be high, fuel costs would also be minimized. Trinity House and other major lighthouse authorities regularly review advances in the design of light sources and lens combinations, so as to apply them where possible.

At the present time, light sources vary a good deal in size and type. Very few lighthouses still retain the 3 ton Fresnel lens assemblies floating on a mercury bath and these will be replaced as re-equipment and automation proceeds. Automation also demands that the light source has a minimum life of a year, so that for greater safety the light bulb can be replaced every six months during routine maintenance. Mercury vapour lamps (Metallarc) have this sort of specification and may replace the old types of filament lamp, the life of which is less easily predictable. This sort of unpredictability is not so important in a manned lighthouse, but it becomes quite unacceptable for an automatic light.

Sealed-beam light assembly on turntable. (AB Pharos Marine Ltd)

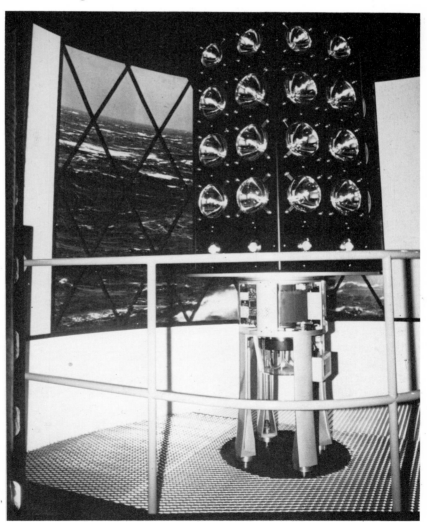

Aga automatic light changer. (AB Pharos Marine Ltd)

Since Winstanley's candle light on the Eddystone Rock shone forth in 1698 as the first regularly lit wave-washed rock in the world, that danger has been almost continuously marked for some 280 years. Lighthouse keepers have watched over the Eddystone, and some have lost their lives in the service of the world's shipping. Thus, it must seem sad that after such a long and honourable history the Eddystone Light should have become fully automatic in 1982. This was just one hundred years since the Douglass structure, the fourth in a famous line of lighthouses on these rocks, had been lit.

The last keepers were withdrawn in July 1981, and while the new equipment was being installed a lightship and buoy were moored nearby as temporary navigation aids. The materials for the new installation were brought by ship and lifted by helicopter to the helideck above the lantern, where a temporary crane was fixed to lower the equipment through the lantern roof. One particularly heavy diesel generator had to be lowered down the outside of the tower so that it could be taken in through the original entrance door. Miles of new electric cabling with sophisticated control panels were fitted and every powered system was duplicated. The monitoring and control system at Penlee Point south of Plymouth is designed so that the function of each

Building the helideck above the lantern of the Bishop Rock Lighthouse in 1976. (Trinity House)

system (lights, fog signal and radiobeacon) can be monitored continuously. Telemetric controls, similar to those used for orbiting spacecraft, enable the shore crew to control the functions if an unforeseen fault in the automatic mechanism should develop. Besides the navaids the tower has automatic fire detection and extinguishing devices.

Two other recent English conversions to automation will be described. The Beachy Head Light, which was transferred from the clifftop to an underwater reef at the foot of the famous white cliffs in 1902, became fully automatic in July 1983. The new equipment is powered by mains electricity passing through twin cables connecting a substation on the top of the cliff with the light tower. A land-line has also been provided to connect the light and other navaids to a control panel in the regional monitoring station at the North Foreland Lighthouse. A standby diesel generator is ready to start up automatically if there is any electricity supply failure. Its fuel is provided from a header tank kept permanently topped up by float switches connected to an electric pump which can draw oil from the main tanks in the base of the tower. The optic is rotated by electric motors with hydraulic drive and the illuminant is a 400W Metalarc

lamp which needs to be changed only at six-monthly intervals. Light output from the lamp and the optic rotation speed are continuously monitored at North Foreland. A third standby ready for use in the unlikely event of the primary and secondary power supplies failing is a sealed-beam rotating beacon powered by batteries kept charged to a level allowing twenty-four hours' operation.

A nautophone fog signal is controlled by a fog detector. This emits a series of flashes and by measuring the quantum of light reflected back to the instrument from the drops of moisture in the atmosphere it can predict the range of visibility and so activate the fog signal at the predetermined level. There is also a comprehensive fire detection and extinguishing system which can automatically release halon gas.

Some automatic lights, particularly minor ones on the French Atlantic coast, have battery powered electric illumination with wind

generators to top up the batteries. A recently installed automatic station on the top of the Nab Tower in the approaches to Portsmouth and Southampton also has four wind generators to top-up a bank of rechargeable batteries, though in calm conditions a propane gas-fuelled generator can cut in. The optic on the Nab Tower is of glass-reinforced plastic and weighs only 450kg. The incandescent light source is fuelled by acetylene gas under pressure which also provides the power to rotate the optic. This Dalen type system is standard equipment for smaller automatic lights.

Many of Britain's famous rock towers have aluminium helipads mounted above the lantern. These spoil their looks, but make them much easier to relieve and service. Repair gangs or inspecting engineers can be flown to the towers in all but the worst weather. The usual design on isolated towers such as the Bishop and the Wolf is a light-metal platform similar to that used on warships, braced to the top of the lantern by struts fixed into the masonry of the tower. Stores and personnel must descend through a trap in the deck to a metal ladder leading to the lantern gallery. On some rock sites an area close to the base of the tower has been prepared as a landing pad. The site of Stevenson's old building barrack on Skerryvore was conveniently available.

Lighthouses built on new sites, such as Tater Du near Land's End in Cornwall and the more recent lights in the Shetlands established for the large ships using the Sullom Voe oil terminal, were designed *de novo* as automatic stations. They are equipped with primary, secondary and tertiary light systems and all possible navaids outside the visual spectrum. As we have seen, the smaller, more intense light sources and the lighter and smaller optics made of moulded glass and polycarbonate allow the modern lighthouse to operate economically with very high luminous efficiency. A great advance in lighthouse illumination has been the use of the sealed-beam light. Since 1960, several new lights have been fitted with arrays of these comparatively cheap units which can have an intermediate range of visibility and are also extremely useful for sector lights and leading lights in harbour entrances.

The French have been very active in the use of wind-generated power for minor lights, and many other countries are experimenting with wind-generated electricity for isolated beacon towers and minor lights. The problems encountered are mainly due to the inevitable turbulence around the light structure. The two- or three-bladed propellers so far designed are not sturdy enough to withstand the exceptional forces to which they are exposed on sea-girt rocks. The blades are designed to feather as the wind strength increases, but despite this propeller and bearing damage is still liable to occur. Thus until better designs are found it is unlikely that many authorities will move over to wind generation on a large scale. The methods of electricity storage from wind power have been well tested and have proved satisfactory, however.

The modern automatic lighthouse, lightship or Lanby is usually equipped with an electrically powered sound signal emitting three tones which is either controlled by nearby shore monitors or by fog detectors, as described earlier. Most are also fitted with racon radar enhancers; these are activated by the radar signal from an approaching ship and send back a strong signal which appears on the ship's screen as a bright blip. In congested waters where pilots could confuse two neighbouring racons, a more sophisticated system can operate whereby each one responds to the ship's radar by an identifying letter which appears as a Morse-coded blip.

Radio communication with remote lighthouses, such as the Flannans, Butt of Lewis, Smalls and Fastnet, was first established before the First World War, and by the 1920s most major lighthouses could communicate by radiotelephone with the shore and passing ships. In 1929 radiobeacons were established at Kinnaird Head and

A racon responder emitter.
(AB Pharos Marine Ltd)

Sule Skerry, and more stations were adapted. These beacons broadcast identifying letters in Morse followed by a loud monotone which can be picked up by a ship within a specified distance, usually about 25 miles. The bearing of the beacon can be found by the ship's radio operator using a simple radio receiver fitted with a magnetic compass. The cross-bearings of two or more signals give a position fix in any condition of visibility.

In 1929, in the early days of radiobeacons, the Little Cumbrae Lighthouse at the entrance to the Clyde broadcast both a sound and radio signal, so timed that, by measuring the time between the reception of each, the ship's pilot could obtain his distance from the lighthouse as well as the bearing. The 'talking beacon' originated with Charles and D. Alan Stevenson and was perfected with the help of the Marconi Co. It soon spread to Europe and North America, where 20 years later there were 74 such beacons, though still only two in Britain, both installed by the Clyde Lighthouse Trustees.

However, while much of the operation of light and broadcast radio aids on lighthouses and lightships can now be carried out by remote control, the international trend towards automation involves the loss of two functions which require manning. These are the visual lookout and the radio watch for vessels in difficulty or distress, and the loss of these has caused considerable heart-searching. Those countries having unified arrangements for navaids, sea rescue and contraband control, such as Canada and the USA, are in some respects better able to meet mariners' needs, but the experienced lookout and radio watchkeeper, perhaps able to pick up signals not detectable by the remoter control

The new automatic light on North Rona some 40 miles northwest of the Scottish mainland. (Stuart Murray)

centre and often stationed in areas of difficult navigation or rough conditions, is still valuable today.

One consequence of the increasing use of radio and radar by ships, lighthouses and coastal surveillance centres is that the maritime authorities of any advanced nation can receive extensive information about ships approaching or leaving their coasts. With nearly fifty per cent of lighthouses now automated, and with many important buoys and Lanbys emitting sound signals, radar reflections or signals and sometimes coded radar identification signals, the pilot of today has little excuse for losing his way.

However, the congestion of certain 'narrow seas' and the size, speed, poor manoeuvrability and long stopping distances of modern bulk carriers pose new problems and dangers. As the chief of these is collision, the function of the seamarks of today has been extended to the shepherding and disciplining of traffic. To a certain extent, the age-long autonomy of the ship's captain has been abrogated by the greater imperative of channel discipline. This so-called autonomy has in any case already been progressively diminished by course and speed orders which are sent out by the owners, who are in possession of commercial and meteorological information not always available to the ship's captain.

The seamarks of the future will still remind the mariner of the dangers of the land and the shoal, but increasingly they will warn him to navigate in accordance with the 'rules of the road' established by international agreement and national authority. This change in emphasis will be the subject of the next and final chapter.

Sources for Chapter XIII

Aids to Navigation 1984–85, Aga Navigation Aids Ltd, Brentford, UK
R. W. Munro
Northern Lighthouse Board technical information
Sjohistorisk Årbok 1942
K. Sutton-Jones
Trinity House technical information, and *Flash Yearbook* 1984

XIV

The Present and the Future of Seamarking

The International Dictionary of Aids to Marine Navigation defines seamarking as an ensemble of beacons, buoys, seamarks and small lights to assist the safe and easy movement of ships. The problems of today and the future put the emphasis on that 'safe and easy movement', the marshalling and control of sea traffic especially in narrow or congested waterways and in harbour entrances, and exact pin-pointing of vessels working from the coast or requiring assistance when in distress.

The concept of seamarking must therefore today be widened to include not only those marks visible to the eye but also those which can be detected on board by electronic means or by sound. We therefore arrive at a concept of the fixed navigational aid or navaid, and from this concept to that of the monitoring centre ashore which collates information about ship movements from a variety of sources, principally radar scanning and radiotelephony, and then relays back to the ship's master his exact position, routeing and traffic advice, and urgent warnings when he is standing into danger.

The master of a ship on the high seas is no longer as independent as he was in the days of James Cook, but he is still just as dependent on the sophisticated seamarking of today. The analogy of air traffic control, or even road traffic control, is obvious. The former demands total compliance from the air-pilot in matters such as flight altitude and the course and timing of airport approach, and radio beacons are placed to keep the flight paths defined and predictable. In the control of sea traffic, shore centres are in some ways faced with greater difficulties than those of air traffic controllers. Although the speed of ships is so much slower, they can move only in a single horizontal plane and are not bound to obey the advice or instructions of the controllers. The large ship takes a long time to stop and can turn only in a wide circle. The authority of shore controllers becomes stronger as a ship enters the confines of a harbour: not only is a pilot aboard, whose allegiance is to the port authorities, but the port has strong legal sanctions to back its authority over the incoming ship.

This is not the case in congested shipping lanes. However, the wide measure of international agreement on the principles of sea traffic control, the sanctions which owners or marine insurers can put on a ship's master, and the sheer powers of persuasion of the shore controllers who in some countries are reinforced by legal sanctions, are succeeding in educating the mariner of today in the importance of channel discipline.

Let us therefore examine in some detail the English Channel and southern part of the North Sea, as a good example of a congested waterway.

After the Second World War the extensive minefields which had been laid off the north coast of Holland and in the approaches to the Ems, Weser, Elbe and Eider rivers were a danger not only to coastal shipping but to the heavy deep-sea traffic between the Atlantic and the Baltic. To overcome the problem, a securely swept sea lane 5 nautical miles broad was established from north of Texel to the first Elbe lightship, and marked by a series of fairway buoys about 4 miles apart. The tall pillar buoys with radar reflectors were in mid-channel so that all ships had to pass to starboard of them. A 150 mile safe seaway was thus established in which ships could expect very little crossing traffic and no opposing traffic, provided they kept the fairway buoys on their port hand.

In 1956 a separation zone between incoming and outgoing ships was established in the Straits of Gibraltar which substantially reduced the risk of collision in this important waterway. The Gulf of Suez and the Channel Straits between England and France were obviously crying out for some similar scheme of separation and with the formation of what is now the International Maritime Organization (IMO) it became possible to plan and monitor such schemes, which would be administered by the riparian countries.

Thus, by the late 1960s it was possible to advise all ships leaving Europe for the Atlantic to keep to the English side of the Channel. Inward-bound ships were advised to follow the French coast: Ushant, Casquets, Cotentin Peninsula, Pas de Calais. Buoyage and lightship guidance was to follow, and the problems of intersecting ferry traffic, inshore vessels and outward bound traffic from the Seine and its associated ports were left.

The present-day solution, as anyone can understand who studies the charts of the English Channel, is that an inshore shipping zone extending 5 miles from a line drawn from headland to headland is established on both sides. In these zones, coastal traffic can pass in either direction. Major Europe-bound traffic coming from the Bay of Biscay or the Western Atlantic is expected to reach a point 10 miles northwest of Ushant and then to follow a course which will clear all headlands of the French coast and Channel Islands by 5 miles. Northwest of the Casquets, the Channel Lightship is stationed to denote the commencement of the formal separation zone between inward and outward bound traffic. From this point the limits of the separation zone are marked by lightships and Lanbys until the difficult narrow section between Dungeness and Calais is reached. Here, the

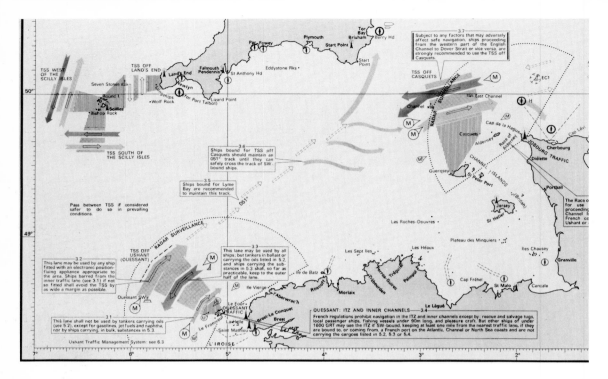

Varne Bank Lightship and buoys, as well as the East Channel Lanby, keep the converging lanes apart while the cross-Channel ferry traffic threads its way across the lanes between the South Goodwin and Varne Lightships. Outward bound traffic from Dunkirk and the Schelde is marshalled well east of the narrows before steering for the west-going route south of Dover, and at this point there has to be continual intersection of traffic inward bound to Rotterdam Europort and the outward bound traffic from Belgium and Dunkerque. The movements of ships are carefully monitored by shore stations on the Pas de Calais, and on the English side pilots are warned of other major traffic movements so that they can take avoiding action according to the Collision Rules in good time.

If we then follow the main route northeast from the East Goodwins Lightship towards Europort and Texel, we find the same principles applied of separated inward and outward bound traffic routes with strategically placed lightships at all bends in the channel or at points of shoal danger. Lightships marking such course changes have the strongest possible radio beacons, and maximum range of light visibility.

On the French side of the English Channel, the master control station is at Ushant, and Corsen on the mainland opposite the island. Here most incoming ships are identified, their destinations ascertained if possible, and the captains warned of any navigational hazards ahead. Secondary stations on the Cotentin Peninsula and at Cape Gris Nez receive full information from the Corsen–Ushant complex about

ABOVE AND RIGHT
Traffic regulation in the English Channel. (Reproduced from British Admiralty Chart 5500 'Mariners' Routeing Guide' with the kind permission of the Controller of H. M. Stationery Office and of the Hydrographer of the Navy)

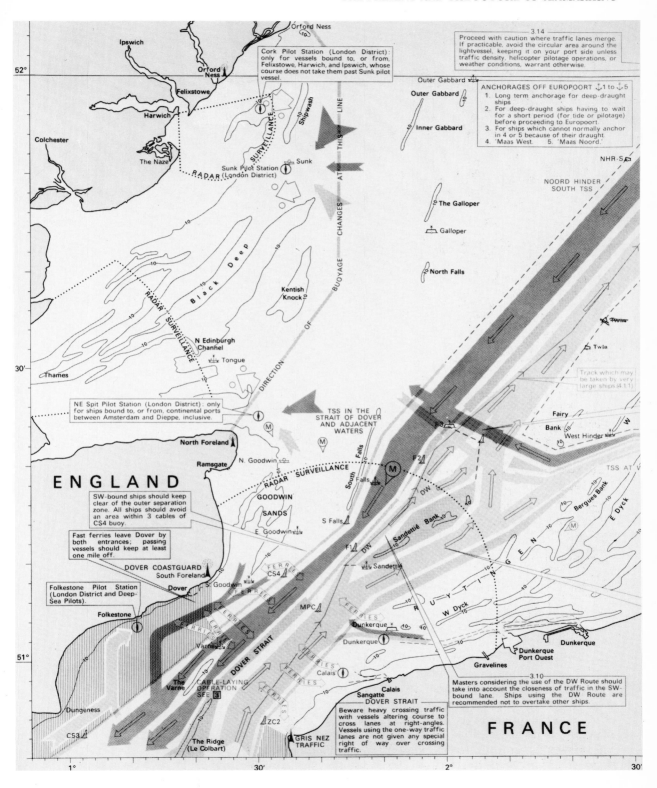

Ipswich

Orford Ness

52°

Orford Ness

Felixstowe

Cork Pilot Station (London District): only for vessels bound to, or from, Felixstowe, Harwich, and Ipswich, whose course does not take them past Sunk pilot vessel.

Harwich

Colchester

The Naze

Shipwash

SURVEILLANCE

Outer Gabbard

Outer Gabbard

Inner Gabbard

3.14
Proceed with caution where traffic lanes merge. If practicable, avoid the circular area around the lightvessel, keeping it on your port side unless traffic density, helicopter pilotage operations, or weather conditions, warrant otherwise.

ANCHORAGES OFF EUROPOORT ⚓1 to ⚓5
1. Long term anchorage for deep-draught ships
2. For deep-draught ships having to wait for a short period (for tide or pilotage) before proceeding to Europoort.
3. For ships which cannot normally anchor in 4 or 5 because of their draught.
4. 'Maas West.   5. 'Maas Noord.'

RADAR

Sunk Pilot Station
(London District)

Sunk

NHR-S

NOORD HINDER
SOUTH TSS

The Galloper

Galloper

Black Deep

Kentish
Knock

North Falls

BUOYAGE CHANGES AT THIS LINE

RADAR SURVEILLANCE

N Edinburgh
Channel

Tongue

Thames

30'

DIRECTION OF

Twin

Twin

Track which may be taken by very large ships (4.1.1)

NE Spit Pilot Station (London District): only for ships bound to, or from, continental ports between Amsterdam and Dieppe, inclusive.

TSS IN THE
STRAIT OF DOVER
AND ADJACENT
WATERS

Fairy
Bank

West Hinder

North Foreland

Ramsgate

N. Goodwin

RADAR SURVEILLANCE

South
Falls

F2

TSS AT

ENGLAND

SW-bound ships should keep clear of the outer separation zone. All ships should avoid an area within 3 cables of CS4 buoy.

GOODWIN
SANDS

South
Falls

M

Bergues Bank

E Dyck

Fast ferries leave Dover by both entrances; passing vessels should keep at least one mile off.

E Goodwin

S Falls

Sandettié Bank

DOVER COASTGUARD
South Foreland

Folkestone Pilot Station (London District and Deep-Sea Pilots).

Dover

S. Goodwin

CS4

FERRIES

F1

DW

Sandettié

W Dyck

R U Y T I N G E N

Folkestone

MPC

Dunkerque

Dunkerque

Dunkerque

Dunkerque
Port Ouest

FERRIES

Varne

Calais

Gravelines

51°

The Varne

CABLE-LAYING
OPERATION
SEE 3

FERRIES

Calais
Sangatte

3.10
Masters considering the use of the DW Route should take into account the closeness of traffic in the SW-bound lane. Ships using the DW Route are recommended not to overtake other ships.

Dungeness

CS3

The Ridge
(Le Colbart)

ZC2

GRIS NEZ
TRAFFIC

DOVER STRAIT
Beware heavy crossing traffic with vessels altering course to cross lanes at right-angles. Vessels using the one-way traffic lanes are not given any special right of way over crossing traffic.

FRANCE

1°   30'   2°   30'

Maritime surveillance tower on the island of Quessant (Ushant). The control centre is on the nearby mainland of Brittany at Corsen. (Commission des Phares et Balises)

incoming ships and they continue to monitor and advise the traffic as it approaches the Straits of Dover.

When the system was first put into full operation in 1979, which was shortly after the *Amoco Cadiz* disaster near Ushant, the number of ships contravening traffic regulations and navigational warnings was very large, but each successive year has seen a steady fall in the number of offenders. Major transgressors over these years have been ships flying flags of convenience, whose masters, perhaps, are not so subject to the discipline of strong national martime authorities. There have also been difficulties in mutual understanding between ship and shore. Nevertheless, the facts show that ships of all flags are increasingly obedient to the internationally accepted traffic regulations and to the warnings of shore controllers. The process of persuading ships' masters to make their historic autonomy subject to the general welfare is proceeding so satisfactorily that it may be unnecessary for the maritime nations to agree on some form of international sanction for the maverick sea captain. The Ushant Regional Operational Centre reported 3,668 contraventions in 1979, but only 991 in 1982. Contraventions noted by the Griz Nez surveillance centre in the period 1975–8 before the separation zone was finally marked off averaged 8,146 annually, whereas in the four subsequent years 1979–83 the contraventions were successively 3,991, 3,221, 2,639 and 2,120. Many of the Calais area culprits are 'crossing ships' disobeying the regulation which requires them to intersect the main traffic lanes at right angles. Contraventions recorded by the Cotentin Surveillance Centre had fallen by 1982 to the very low figure of 382. It therefore seems as if, with a steady annual regression of infringements, a time will soon come when all but a few ships will obey marine traffic regulations without

Table to show the secular trend in the contraventions of traffic control regulations as monitored off Ushant, in the central English Channel and in the Pas de Calais. (Commission des Phares et Balises)

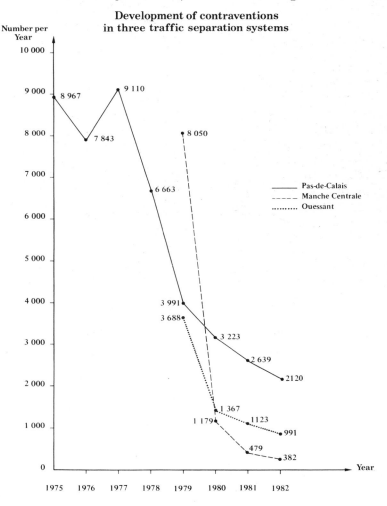

Development of contraventions in three traffic separation systems

trouble or difficulty. Already, more than half of the contravening ships can be identified by the French authorities; they are then reported to their owners' countries for any further action.

In entering major estuaries to proceed to their destinations upriver, large ships have little room for error. Traditional seamarking has hitherto been adequate for the experienced pilot, but new systems have been developed which will direct the ship along the best channel with great accuracy. The Sarel system installed in the channel of the Loire in the approaches to St Nazaire is a modification of the Syledis radio location system which is widely used. Transmitting radio beacons set up on either side of the river send pulses towards a ship, which returns them to the shore stations, thereby transmitting information on her position, course and speed. This data is computed at a calculation centre and then relayed back to the ship with a delay of a few seconds. It also appears on a recording centre in the harbour master's office. A comparable system has been installed in the Garonne. The Syledis system, with various modifications, has also been widely used in oil drilling, aerial and marine surveying and pipe-laying. The combination of spaced radio emitters and responders allows very exact placement of an interrogating ship.

A world-wide system of hyperbolic position fixing known as Omega depends on a network of transmitting beacons along the coasts. To cater for the great accuracy of position required by fishing trawlers, subsidiary systems such as Toran and Rana P17 have been set up by French maritime authorities.

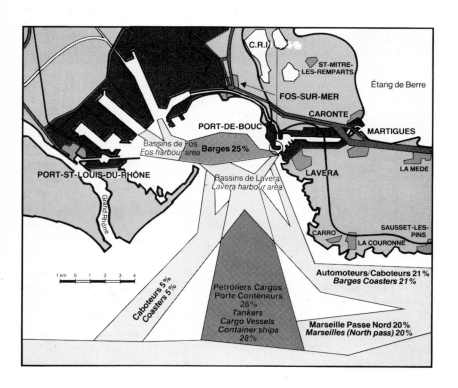

The density and complexity of ship traffic entering a major port is indicated by this diagram of the Golfe de Fos, just west of Marseilles. Surveillance and control is done by the Integrated Traffic Regulation Centre (CRI) at Port de Bouc, where the harbour master, pilotage and towage services are also on permanent duty. The approach radar from the aerials on top of Cap Couronne lighthouse is relayed to the CRI control centre at Port de Bouc, which also has its own high-definition, shorter range radars. The control room is at the top of a 25m tower, and combines the functions of visual and radar observation with VHF radio, radar transceiver, telex and telephone communications.

Le Havre Port Control centre, at the entrance to the port.

Many ships today rely for position-fixing on satellite navigation (Satnav) systems, but as there is some delay in obtaining the readings the position of automated lightships cannot yet be monitored in this way. However, as they are generally not very far offshore other very accurate continuous means such as Decca can be used.

All major ports have extensive radar scanning facilities; information is fed into the port control centre so that the movement of ships can be harmonised and the pilots given instructions as to route and berthing destination. Such rapidly changing monitoring and direction facilities cannot really be included in the category of seamarking, for they involve vessels in accepting orders from shore and being compelled to wait before moving. This time factor cannot be controlled by conventional seamarks, except in the use of traffic light signals for entry into docks and locks. The modern requirement is overwhelmingly for 'safe and easy movement', and since the older type of seamark cannot guarantee this, the new systems of port control are increasingly taking over.

Lighthouse authorities throughout the world are under continuous pressure from shipowners to reduce the charges for their service. The cost to the shipowner is, broadly speaking, related to the tonnage of the vessel, and the larger ships which pay the most are those most completely equipped with intrinsic navigational aids such as sophisticated radar and computerised displays derived from satellite, Omega, Decca and depth-monitoring inputs. Naturally, therefore, the spokesmen for those big-ship owners press the point that fixed visual and sound aids (and sometimes radiobeacons) are something they can do without. To paraphrase the words of a famous courtesan, 'they would say that'. However, lighthouse authorities have to consider the whole broad spectrum of maritime interests: the yachtsmen, the inshore fishermen, dredgers and small coasters as well as the 'big boys'. There is also the overall consideration of safety at sea: not only does the absence of any need for on-board equipment make the older visual and sound seamarks unique and invaluable to the self-sufficient vessel, but there is always the real possibility of failure, malfunction or misinterpretation of other systems, all of which are electrically powered and electronic in nature. The very positive values of simplicity with precision, and independence of complex equipment, remain relevant. Where the service is funded from central government, necessary capital developments are restrained and often impeded by the conflicting demands of other public works, but on the other hand government is in a position to see that all the user interests contribute in some way to the cost of providing fixed navigational aids. High costs of revenue collection can be entailed if direct charges are levied on all users including pleasure boats and foreign craft, however.

In Britain, where Trinity House, under the supervision and control of the Department of Transport, pays for the service from the General Lighthouse Fund and where light cargo-carrying dues are levied only on vessels over 20 tons, it can be argued that there is a whole range of users who do not contribute to the cost of the service. If those who pay the piper call the tune, there is a risk that the present 'Rolls-Royce' service might in the future be curtailed to the ultimate detriment of safety and the marine environment. Perhaps some more equitable sharing of costs can be devised which will not limit or constrain the ultimate ideal of making our sea coasts as safe as possible for the mariner. It is inconceivable that the sailor, especially the small craft man, will ever be able to do without the traditional seamarks – the buoys, the beacons, leading marks, sector lights and landfall lights. From the first birch branch stuck in the mud on the bend of a river, they have served sailors well and saved countless lives. We are not likely to abandon them.

Sources for Chapter XIV

Surveillance of Port and Maritime Navigation. Recent French Achievements. Ministere de la Mer, Paris.
Corsen-Ouessant Regional Operational Centre for Surveillance and Rescue. Ministere de la Mer, Paris.

APPENDIX A

Some Notes on the Administration of Lighthouse and Seamarking Services

In the various countries of the world different methods developed of financing and administering fixed navigational aids, and in many countries the methods changed over the years. In the United States coast lighting was at first in the charge of local colonial governments, then centralized federally under the Secretary of the Treasury, had a period under naval and military control, and finally came under the wing of the Coast Guard. However, the funding and role of this service are now under review by the US government.

The French Service has always been centralized, at first rather weakly so under Royal decrees and then very firmly under the Republican Ministry of Public Works, which included a special department (Ponts et Chausées) devoted to the civil engineering of canals, bridges, and harbours. The Service des Phares et Balises became partly autonomous early in the nineteenth century but has always had to compete for funds with other public works. It is now under the Ministry of Transport.

Previously, colonial countries have tended to follow the pattern established by their original occupying power. Thus, most of the French former colonies in North Africa have a service of Phares et Balises or of Signalisation Maritime. The Philippines follow American practice with a Coast Guard. Australia and New Zealand have their Lighthouse Service under the Minister of Transport, as in the U.K., although the British lighthouses together with the Merchant Marine had a long period under the control of the Board of Trade in the nineteenth and early twentieth centuries. Spanish American and many Comecon countries combine their lighthouse administration with their naval hydrographic services, thus linking coastal safety with defence. The Japanese have a specific Maritime Safety Agency.

Below are listed some examples of the different controlling agencies for lighthouse services:

Centralized Service under Ministry of Public Works or Transport: France, former colonies of France

Ancient Corporations or Commissions under Department or Ministry of Transport: England, Scotland, Ireland

Department under Ministry of Transport: Australia, S Africa, W
Germany
Part of Naval Hydrographic Service: Most Spanish American
countries, German Democratic Republic
Part of Ministry of Shipping and/or Maritime Affairs: Netherlands,
Poland
Part of Coast Guard Service: U.S.A., Canada, Philippines
Maritime Safety Agency: Japan
Port Authorities: Many smaller countries
Department of Lighthouses and Lightships: India
Joint Service of several adjoining countries: Middle East Navigational
Aid Service (MENAS)

FINANCE

The cost of a lighthouse service clearly depends to a large extent on the
length and nature of the coastline and the complexity and difficulty of
its coastal seaways. Some countries such as Britain, which stand
athwart the seaways leading from the Southern and Western
Hemispheres into the great European ports of the North Sea and the
Baltic, provide navigation services and aids used by ships from all over
the world. Denmark, Norway, Sweden and the Arabian Gulf States are
in a similar relationship to world shipping. To a certain extent all
countries provide for passing ships as well as those making for their own
ports.

Because of this element of universal service, the custom developed in
early times of ships paying dues according to the number of lights they
had passed on their voyage. Perhaps the earliest example of this
systematic taxing were the Sound Dues payable to the Crown of
Denmark by all ships passing through the narrows east of Elsinore and
Copenhagen. Great Britain consolidated its many and various Light
Dues in 1898 and established a General Lighthouse Fund derived from
tonnage of the vessel (reflecting her value and earning potential) and
the number of voyages rather than the number of lighthouses passed.

In this system, ships pay on an annually adjusted scale which is based
on the amount needed to finance the Lighthouse Authorities.
Payments are per 10 tons of registered tonnage per voyage, but there
are different rates for home trade sailing ships, home trade steamers,
foreign-going sailing ships, foreign-going steamers and visiting cruise
ships. No ship pays for more than fourteen voyages a year and foreign-
going steamers who pay the maximum rate are charged for only seven
voyages a year. There are many exceptions including fishing and naval
vessels, dredgers and sailing boats under 100 tons. Annual rates are
decided by Parliament when approving the Estimates of the Minister
of Transport. The Minister of Transport scrutinizes the ten year
forward budget proposals of the various Lighthouse Authorities (for
Scottish and Northern Ireland waters, and Trinity House for England
and Wales), receives advice from shipping interests represented by his
Shipping Advisory Committee, and is able to veto or postpone capital

projects or to put financial pressure on the Authorities to reduce establishments. In such ways their forward planning is constantly exposed to critical scrutiny and the necessities of stringent economy. The tonnage rate eventually agreed is clearly a compromise between what the Authorities believe they need and what the world's shipping is prepared to pay. In 1983–4 the maximum rate for 10 tons per voyage was £2.88, so large sums are involved for the shipping companies. Much reduced rates are paid by cruise ships, tugs, large yachts and pleasure boats.

If the annual expenditure of the British Lighthouse Authorities totals £20 million, this could be expressed as £0.34 per head of population or £164 per square mile of territory. However, a very important factor is the length and complexity of the coastline. Including offshore islands Great Britain and Ireland together have a coastline in excess of 4000 miles so the cost of their lighthouse services is £5000 per mile of coastline per annum. This figure makes the service sound very expensive, which it is, but it takes no account of the really important element in the provision of navaids, which is the density and value of the shipping transversing the coastal seaways. Thus, for example, West Germany has a rather short coastline, but it is hydrographically an extremely complex one with a high shipping density. It needs, therefore, large numbers of buoys, beacons, lighthouses and radio aids.

The General Lighthouse Fund is not shared with the Port and Local Authorities who install and maintain navaids in harbours and certain other locally defined waters or for the use of local vessels; e.g. Mersey Docks and Harbour Board. Though such work is subject to the approval of Trinity House it is not at its expense, and the local Authorities and Harbour Commissioners rely on income from property rates and harbour dues.

In smaller countries away from the main shipping channels navaids are administered by the Port Authorities. Where a number of countries have a coastline forming the borders of an international seaway it has proved feasible to set up a joint authority to provide navaids, the National Port Authorities contributing their financial quota to the joint service. At the Straits of Hormuz the Middle East Navigation Aids Service or MENAS, whose executive base is at Bahrain and whose registered office is in London, has developed a highly sophisticated and cost-efficient service which is well respected by international shipping.

Large centralized services such as Phares et Balises based in Paris draw their funds from general taxation in which of course Customs and harbour revenues are included. The same applies to those countries where the service is provided by a Ministry of Marine or of Shipping, by a Coast Guard or by the Hydrographic Department of a Ministry of Defence. The simplicity of drawing funds from central sources is to some extent offset by the conflicting claims of other public works and services which in times of national economic stringency may lead to the postponement of much-needed improvements. The direct contribution of foreign shipping to a country's lighthouse service can only be through charges collected at the ports, although this only affects vessels that call there and not those passing the coast, though they make use of much of the same navigation and safety services.

As a footnote to these notes on finance, the IALA bulletin of 1983–4 includes an analysis of the sources of income of constituent members. Although not all Authorities responded to the questionnaires sent out, the present position seems to be that somewhat over half of all the Authorities derive their income from Light, Port and Pilotage Dues, about a quarter from general taxation and the remainder from mixed sources.

Throughout the world, but excluding China and the USSR who have not provided statistics, there appear to be about 20,000 personnel employed in lighthouse services of which a quarter are established and professional staff, a quarter employed in buoy and lighthouse tenders, and half employed as lightkeepers or maintenance staff.

A good example of a large country with a long but reasonably straightforward coastline is Brazil, which employs about 150 established staff, 250 lighthouse keepers, etc and 275 crew of tenders. Comparable rounded figures for France are 200, 600 and 300. These higher figures reflect the great complexity of the French coastline and the higher concentration of shipping along its coasts.

Most Authorities maintain both large and small vessels to service their navaids, many have a variety of land vehicles, and a few have helicopters and other aircraft available. Although the Canadian Authority deploys some 35 helicopters these are used for a variety of Coast Guard functions and not solely for lighthouse servicing. England makes do with two and Scotland with one helicopter solely employed in servicing remote lighthouses and lightships. Helicopter servicing is manpower efficient, but very expensive.

Most major lighthouse Authorities engage in research and development work; assessing and evaluating scientific advances in illumination, projection, energy sources and electronic control. Much is also done by major commercial suppliers. All authorities report to IALA a gradual change from manned to unmanned, and from visual to non-visual, navaids within the past decade. Each year a larger number of highly trained maintenance engineers and electronic specialists are employed while the number of temporary or vocationally trained staff declines.

APPENDIX B

Marking for Offshore Installations

Extracts from the international regulations as introduced in May 1984.

IALA rules provide for the marking of isolated obstructions to navigation such as wrecks, but the rapid growth of oil exploratory and extraction structures either moored to or fixed to the seabed has led Lighthouse Authorities to draw up special regulations which have to be followed by the oil companies raising such obstructions, and of which mariners are fully informed. The arrangements for marking and lighting the platforms are the responsibility of the oil companies, but are subject to the inspection of the relevant Lighthouse Aurhority. Rigs under tow are marked according to the International Regulations for Avoiding Collisions at Sea.

SECTION A—STRUCTURE (OR VESSEL)

1. MAIN LIGHT(S)

(a) A flashing White light (or lights operated in unison) to exhibit Morse letter **U** every 15 seconds. . . .

(b) The light(s) shall normally be mounted at not less than 12 metres and not more than 30 metres above MHWS (sea level in the case of floating rigs or vessels) and shall be arranged so that an unobstructed flashing White light is visible in any direction.

(c) The apparent intensity of each light after all losses including lantern glazing etc have been taken into account is to be not less than 12,000 candela. The beam axis shall be directed so that it is not elevated above the horizontal or depressed below the horizon. The total beamwidth in the vertical plane shall be not less than 2.5° at the points on the curve of intensity distribution where the intensity is 10% of the maximum.

(d) In exceptional cases where the height of the platform of a permanent structure is such that the main light(s) cannot be mounted below 30 metres, they may be mounted at a height above MHWS of not more than 35 metres. In such cases the beam axis shall be directed at the horizon.

(e) The light(s) shall be exhibited from 15 minutes before sunset until sunrise and at all times when the meteorological visibility in any direction is 2 miles or less.

(f) All structures (or vessels) shall be equipped with a secondary lighting system to come into operation automatically on failure of the White light(s). The secondary lighting system shall be capable of continuous operation at full power for at least four calendar days (96 hours) from a power source independent of that by which the main light(s) is (are) operated. The secondary light(s) shall exhibit Morse letter **U** every 15 seconds . . . and shall be mounted as required by (b) above and so arranged that an unobstructed flashing White light is visible in any direction. The apparent intensity of each light . . . is to be not less than 1,200 candela.

(g) An alarm signal is to be fitted to the main control room, to give warning to operating personnel should the main lights fail.

2. SUBSIDIARY LIGHTS

(a) Flashing Red lights to exhibit the same character as the main light(s) as described in para 1(a) of this Section; the Red lights to operate in unison with each other (but not necessarily in unison with the main light(s)).

(b) The subsidiary lights are to be so positioned as to mark the horizontal extremities of the structure or vessel except those extremities which may have already been marked by main flashing White lights . . . Each subsidiary light is to provide the maximum arc of illumination possible from its position.

(c) The apparent intensity of each Red light . . . is not to be less than 15 candela. The beam axis shall be directed so that it is not elevated above the horizontal or depressed below the horizon. The total beamwidth in the vertical plane shall be not less than 2.5° at the points on the curve of intensity distribution where the intensity is 10% of the maximum.

(d) The lights shall be exhibited from 15 minutes before sunset until sunrise.

3. FOG SIGNALS

(a) A fog signal (or signals operated in unison) to sound the Morse letter **U** viz:

Blast	0.75 secs	
Silent	1.00 secs	
Blast	0.75 secs	6 secs
Silent	1.00 secs	
Blast	2.50 secs	
Silent	24.00 secs	
Total period	30.00 secs	

(b) The fog signal emitter(s) shall be mounted at not less than 12 metres and not more than 35 metres above MHWS (sea level in the case of floating rigs or vessels) and shall be so arranged that the fog signal shall have a usual range of at least 2 sea miles in any direction.

(c) The fog signal(s) shall be sounded whenever the meteorological visibility in any direction is 2 sea miles or less.

(d) All structures (vessels) shall be equipped with a secondary fog signal system, with a usual range of at least $\frac{1}{2}$ sea mile in any direction. The secondary fog signal, which shall be independent of the main signal, is to come into operation automatically in the event of total failure of the main signal, or if partial failure of the main signal results in the usual range falling below $\frac{1}{2}$ sea mile in any direction.

(e) The main and secondary fog signals shall each be capable of operating continuously at full power for at least four calendar days (96 hours) from a power source independent of the main supply.

[*fig omitted*]

4. IDENTIFICATION PANELS

(a) Identification panels are to display the registered name or other designation of the structure (vessel) in black letters/figures 1 metre high on a yellow background and shall be so arranged that at least one panel is visible from any direction.

(b) The panels are to be illuminated. Alternatively, the letters/figures are to be on a retro-reflective background.

SECTION B—MOORINGS AND BUOYS

Any unlighted buoys attached to the moorings of a structure shall be coloured Dayglow Yellow (existing buoys may continue to be coloured Orange while stocks last). The buoys shall carry on their sides identification markings indicating the ownership of the installation or the name of the operating company. The characters used shall be as large as the size of the buoy allows.

SECTION C—MARKING IN THE EVENT OF TOTAL FAILURE OF THE NAVIGATIONAL AIDS

If at any time there should be a total failure of the navigational aids, both primary and secondary, fitted to a structure, temporary marking shall be established at the earliest possible moment. Immediate temporary marking shall be *either by*:

The establishment of two Cardinal light buoys on opposite sides of the structure and one cable from it. Each light buoy to be fitted with the appropriate topmark, a radar reflector and a fog signal to be either a wave-actuated bell, a wave-actuated whistle, or an electronic bell or electric fog signal with a character of one stroke/blast every 5 seconds and a usual range of at least 0.5 sea miles . . . The buoy lights to have an apparent intensity, after all losses including lantern glazing etc have been taken into account, of not less than 70 candela . . .

or A transportable battery-operated package to be placed on the structure itself and consisting of a light having the characteristics set out in Section A1 (f) above and a fog signal with the characteristics set out in Section A3 (a) to (c) above.

The above represents the minimum immediate standard requirements. Additional marking may subsequently be specified by the Department [of Transport].

NOTES
4. Nothing in this marking schedule shall affect the requirement for all vessels to comply with the relevant rules of the International Regulations for the Prevention of Collisions at Sea.
5. The characteristics of Cardinal buoys shall be in accordance with the IALA Maritime Buoyage system.

Annotated Bibliography

Adams, W. H. D. *Lighthouses and Lightships*. Nelson, London, 1878. A dated book with some doubtful historical facts.

Allard, Emile *Les Phares, Histoire, Construction, Éclairage*. Rothschild, Paris, 1889. A huge and liberally illustrated book, no expense spared by Rothschild, weighing over 15 kg and quite unsuitable for a normal library shelf. It gives a vivid picture of the French lighthouse service and its achievements in the nineteenth century. The historical notes are valuable but limited to 'Phares et Fanals'. The early history of buoyage in France is not touched on.

Ashley, A. *The Mariner's Mirrour*. London, 1588. English adaptation of Waghenaer's widely used sea charts and sailing directions. Shows the state of buoyage and beaconage at the end of the sixteenth century.

Bailey, John E. *Transcription of the Minutes of the Corporation of Boston 1545–1607*. History of Boston Project, Borough of Boston, Lincolnshire, 1980.

Bedford, G. D. *The Sailor's Pocket Book*. Griffin, Portsmouth, 1874. Short manual for coastwise sailors. Throws light on confusing local systems of buoyage at that time.

Behrmann, Walter *Uber niederdeutschen Seebücher des funfsehnten und sechszehnten Jahrhunderts*, Mitteilungen der Geographischen Gesellschaft in Hamburg. Band XXI. Friedrichsen, Hamburg, 1906. Sets out the correspondences and divergences of the sailing directions given in Low German Seebüchs as compared with Italian Portolanos and French Sea Routiers. The evidence suggests that German and Flemish pilots were constantly exchanging information with the French and Italians.

Blaeu, W. J. *Light of Navigation*, Amsterdam, 1612. *The Sea Mirror*, Ansterdam, 1612. Both series of charts give a visual picture of the state of seamarking in North Europe at the end of the sixteenth century.

Board of Trade, England *Historical Notes on Uniform Buoyage*, 1933. Paper available from Trinity House, London.

Bowen, F. *The Work of Trinity House, Shipping Wonders of the World*, ed. C. Winchester. The Fleetway House, London, 1936. An accurate general survey of Trinity House history.

Carlson, V. *Maritime Telegraph Systems, Buoys, Beacons, etc*. Stockholm, 1890.

Collins, Greenvile *Great Britain's Coasting Pilot*. Harrap, London, 1753. A re-issue of the published charts, silhouettes and directions resulting from Collin's late seventeenth century surveys.

Crommelin, L. and van Suchtelen, H. *Nederlandse vuurtorens: bougeschedenis en organatie*. Neeuwkoop, Heuff, 1978. A good account of Holland's lighthouses, but not much information on other seamarks.

Defoe, D. *The Tour through the Whole Island of Great Britain, 1727*. Penguin, London, 1981. Invaluable insight into trade and transportation in early eighteenth century.

Denham, H. M. *Denham's Mersey and Dee Navigation*. Mawdsley, Liverpool, 1840. A rather jumbled account of the improvements made by Liverpool's greatest Hydrographer and Engineer. Describes the Mitchell Screw Pile Lighthouse at Fleetwood. Charts show Liverpool's very egregious methods of buoyage – immensely complicated.

Dodds, M. H. *The North Shields Lighthouses*. The Priory Press, Tynemouth, 1928. A fascinating account drawn from the books of the Trinity House, Newcastle, of the building and commissioning of Britain's first leading lights. A limited edition of 100 copies.

Edwards, E. P. *Our Seamarks*. Longmans Green, London, 1884. A compilation from a series of articles previously published in the *Nautical Magazine*. Describes the building of a caisson beacon off Margate, and early experiments in buoy lighting.

Elliott, G. H. *European Lighthouse Systems: Being a report of tour of inspection made in 1873*. Washington, 1874. Report of a fact-finding tour, full of technical information on the state of lighthouse engineering towards the end of its era of maximum expansion.

Encyclopedia Brittanica, 11th Ed, 1911, Section on Lighthouses. Lots of facts and figures about nineteenth century lighthouse engineering.

Faille, R. *Les Phares et la signalisation au XVIIe Siecle*. XVIIe Siècle, 86–7, 1970. A good account of ancient French lights.

Forster, E. M. *Pharos and Pharillon*. London, 1925.

Friendly, A. *Beaufort of the Admiralty*. Hutchinson, London, 1960. Useful general background on the links between the Hydrographers of the Admiralty and seamarking in distant waters.

Hague, D. B. *Lighthouses*. Colston Papers, Vol. XXIII.

Hague, D. B. and Christie, R. *Lighthouses: their Architecture, History and Archeology.* Gomer Press, Llandysul, 1975. A masterly account of the history of lighthouse building throughout the world which includes a very clear exposition of the engineering and architectural devices used by the great lighthouse builders. A work of scholarship with an excellent Bibliography and many original drawings by Douglas Hague.

Harris, C. G. *The Trinity House of Deptford, 1514–1660.* The Athlone Press, London, 1969. Useful history of the emergence of the premier Trinity House as a national institution of England. Refers to early buoyage and pilotage problems in the Thames and at Sandwich.

Hazewinkel, H. C. *Een zeldzame prent van J. C. Philips.* 1936, Rotterdams Jaarboekje, p. 55–64. Describes history of leading lights at the mouth of the River Maas and the building of the Steenbake.

Henningsen, H. *Poppinjays and lever lights* in *Det Danske Fyrvaesen 1560–1960.* Yearbook of the Danish Maritime Museum, Kobenhavn, 1960. History of lever lights and early fire towers in Denmark.

Holland, Francis R. *America's Lighthouses 1772 to 1981.* Stephen Greene, Brattleboro, Vermont, 1972. A comprehensive account of the building and administration of lighthouses from colonial days to the present.

Hutchinson, W. *A Treatise on Practical Seamanship.* Published by the author, 1777; republished Scolar Press, London, 1978. A classic work which includes a useful section on Liverpool's early experiments with leading lights, oil lamps and parabolic reflectors.

International Association of Lighthouse Authorities (IALA), 1982. *International Co-operation in Aids to Navigation 1889–1955.* Bibliography of various papers read at PIANC Conferences.

International Dictionary of Aids to Marine Navigation, Vols. I & II.

Jackson, G. *The History and Archaeology of Ports.* World's Work, 1983. Gives the background to the organization of harbour services.

Klessman, K. *Gesichte der Stadt Hamburg.* Hoffmann & Campe, Hamburg, 1981. History of the port and city of Hamburg.

Lang, A. W. *Geschichte des Seezeichenwesens.* Der Bundesminister für Verkehr [Ministry of Transport], Bonn, 1965. A wonderful history, illustrated with many old charts, drawings, prints and documents, concerning the buoyage and beaconage of the German North Sea coast and the mouths of the great rivers up to the mid-1800s. Packed with information obtainable nowhere else, and has a full bibliography of archive sources in the German, Dutch and English literature.

League of Nations Uniform System of Maritime Buoyage, *Texts of draft agreement* . . . Geneva, 1936.

Long, N. *The Lights of East Anglia.* Terence Dalton, Lavenham, 1983. An excellent account of the development of lights along England's most complex coastal sea route. The emphasis is on local history in the age of private lighthouse concessions during the seventeenth and eighteenth centuries, when the Newcastle–London coal trade and the Yarmouth herring fisheries were at their zenith.

Lower, M. A. (ed) *A Survey of the Coast of Sussex made in 1587 with a view to its defence against Foreign Invasion and especially against the Spanish Armada.* Baxter, Lewes, 1870. The maps of Sussex show a whole series of twin beacons on cliff tops, dunes and inland hills.

Luttermann, H. J. and Steinbach, K. *Leuchtfeuer, Tonnen und Baken.* Rostocker Hefte 7, Ostseedruck, Rostock, 1980. A few details on the history of Rostock haven and its seamarks.

Mair, C. *A Star for Seamen: the Stevenson Family of Engineers.* Murray, London, 1978. Very readable biography with much technical information on the Stevensons' works and inventions.

McGrail, S. *The Ship: Rafts, Boats and Ships.* HMSO, London, 1981. Essential background to the development of marine technology in the era of growth of seaborne trade.

Matthews, N. F. Personal communication. He was present at all the committees and working groups of IALA from 1965 to 1980, and was Secretary to Committee A and later Chairman of Committee B.

Meulen, C. van der, Bruynzeel, J. Waaleman and Wallenburg, J. A. van *Wegwijzers op Het Water.* De Boer Maritiem, Unieboek, Bussum, 1978. Good history of pilotage and seamarking in Dutch waters.

Morcken, R. *Europas eldste Sjömerker.* Sjöfartshistorsk Arbok 7–45. Bergen, 1969. An account based on archeological evidence and saga history of Norwegian seamarks erected by the Vikings.

Müller, H-O. *Die Leuchtfeuer von Cuxhaven und Neuwerk.* Koehlers, Herford, 1984. A full history of seamarking at the mouth of the Elbe.

Munro, R. W. *Scottish Lighthouses.* Thule Press, Stornoway, 1979. A well researched and illustrated book with valuable detail on the building of the Bell Rock Light and other famous rock towers, and on the history of the administration and modernization of Scottish lights up to 1978.

Nicholson, C. *Rock Lighthouses of Britain.* Patrick Stephens, Cambridge, 1983. Very well written review of the story of the most famous rock stations in Britain. Brings the story up to date and is superbly illustrated.

Norwich, J. J. *A History of Venice.* Penguin Books, 1983.

Rees, J. S. *History of the Liverpool Pilotage Service.* Southport Guardian, Southport, 1949. Describes the immensely rapid growth of Liverpool seamarking in the eighteenth century.

Report of the Commissioners appointed to enquire into the condition and management of lights, buoys and beacons. Eyre & Spotteswood for HMSO, London, 1861. Contains detailed evidence from mariners and harbour authorities on the state of seamarking at a critical period of maritime expansion, when a method of buoy lighting had not yet been invented and when buoys were immensely variable in construction, shape and topmarking. Illustrates the strong prejudices as well as the immense commonsense of the nineteenth century seaman, and a growing awareness of the need for engineering and hydrographic research.

Report of the Conference appointed to consider the proposal for an uniform system of buoyage for the United Kingdom. Eyre & Spotteswood for HMSO, London, 1883. Britain's first attempt to make some sense of buoy shapes and colours, with the Queen's second son in the chair. It was not very successful, but it was a beginning.

Reynaud, M. L. *Memoire sur l'éclairage et le balisage des cotes de France.* Presse Imperale, Paris, 1864. Allard's predecessor as Chief of the Commission des Phares gives his de luxe account of its achievements since the time of Fresnel.

Ritchie, G. S. *The Admiralty Chart.* Hollis & Carter, London, 1967. Includes some accounts of the erection of seamarks by Admiralty hydrographers in dangerous waters near Britain's colonial possessions.

Robinson, A. H. W. *Marine Cartography in Britain: A History of the Sea Chart to 1855.* Leicester, 1962. Includes Elizabethan charts of Thames Estuary indicating paucity of buoys and beacons.

Sjöhistorisk Arbok 1942, p. 207. German summary of Swedish article on earliest Swedish lighthouses.

Southampton Record Series Port Books and Admiralty Court records.

Stevenson, A. *Skerryvore Lighthouse.* Edinburgh, 1848. A classic by a great Victorian engineer.

Stevenson, D. Alan *The World's Lighthouses Before 1820.* OUP, London, 1959. Taps information from the Stevenson family archives, which makes this an important book of record.

Storey, A. (1) *Trinity House of Kingston-upon-Hull.* Hull, 1967. The records of the Trinity House of Deptford Strond were destroyed by fire, so the Hull records, admirably presented by Storey, are the only surviving documents to show the gradual transition of a Trinity Guild from a primarily religious and charitable body to a working association of master mariners and pilots.

Storey, A. (2) *Hull Trinity House: History of pilotage and navigational aids of the R. Humber 1502–1908.* Ridings Publ. Co., Driffield, 1971. Shows the early struggles of the Hull Trinity House to improve the pilotage of a difficult tidal river, and the comparatively backward state of English methods of buoyage and beaconage in the Tudor era. In the nineteenth century Hull T. H. became a forward-looking buoyage authority which successfully established a whole series of leading lights on the shores of the estuary.

Sutton-Jones, K. *Pharos: the Lighthouse Yesterday, Today and Tomorrow.* Michael Russel, Salisbury, 1985. This recently published book is the definitive guide to modern navigational aids, written by a professional engineer who has spent his whole life in the inspection, design and upgrading of such facilities. It is beautifully illustrated both by photographs and drawings which explain clearly the principles of lighthouse illumination and modern methods of lighthouse and beacon engineering. The author's thoughts about the future of navaids are well worth consideration. The book includes concise biographies of Gustav Dalén and Chance Brothers as well as personal reminiscences of restoring the lights of Borneo after the Second World War and enthusiastic accounts of the Swedish automated system of navaids and of MENAS.

Taylor, E. G. R. *The Haven-finding Art*. Hollis & Carter for the Inst. of Navigation, London, 1956, 1971. Contains much scholarly detail about early navigational advances and sailing directions in the Mediterranean. Good analysis of early Italian Portolanos, notably *Compasso da Navigare*.

Terrell, Christopher Personal communication.

Thompson, P. *History of Boston*. Longman, London, 1856. Records the names and positions of beacons and buoys in approaches to Boston Haven as recorded in a survey of 1580.

Veen, R. van der *Vuurtorens*. De Boer Maritiem, Bussum, 1981. Liberally illustrated history of Dutch lighthouses.

Waghenhaer, L. J. *Karte der Seeküsten Preussens*. Charts of Baltic harbour entrances show early buoyage, fire towers, etc.

Waters, D. W. *The Rutters of the Sea: the Sailing Directions of Pierre Garcie*. Yale University Press, 1967.

Watkins, A. *The Old Straight Track: its Mounds, Beacons and Stones*. Millman, London, 1933. On the basis of careful studies, the author propounds a theory as to how ancient surveyors planned trackways across country and demonstrates how these ley lines can be traced today by observing that fords, cross roads, hilltop markings and large buildings such as churches and towers lie along straight lines.

Wiedemann, G. *International Co-operation in Aids to Navigation 1889–1955*. One of the 'founding fathers' of IALA describes the history of the various conferences which led up to its formation at Scheveningen in 1955. Rich in detail on technical advances of late nineteenth and twentieth century.

Woodman, Richard *Keepers of the Sea*. Terence Dalton, Lavenham, Suffolk, 1983. A serving officer of Trinity House, presently Master of the *Patricia*, tells the story of buoy yachts and steam tenders from the eighteenth century onwards. A very well researched local history which gives a very clear insight into the problems of maintaining seamarks in peace and war.

Zemke, F-K. *Deutsche Leuchttürme, einst und jetzt*. Koehlers, Herford, 1982. An up-to-date historical survey of German lights with very well illustrated documentation of modern seabed light towers in the last twenty years.

Index